PRACTICE MAKES PERFECT

English Pronouns and Prepositions

English Pronouns and Prepositions

Ed Swick

McGraw-Hill

New York   Chicago   San Francisco   Lisbon   London   Madrid   Mexico City
Milan   New Delhi   San Juan   Seoul   Singapore   Sydney   Toronto

2 3 4 5 6 7 8 9 0   CUS/CUS   0 9 8

ISBN 0-07-144775-X
Library of Congress Control Number: 2004115275

McGraw-Hill books are available at special quantity discounts to use as premiums and sales promotions, or for use in corporate training programs. For more information, please write to the Director of Special Sales, Professional Publishing, McGraw-Hill, Two Penn Plaza, New York, NY 10121-2298. Or contact your local bookstore.

This book is printed on acid-free paper.

Contents

Introduction vii

PART I	Pronouns	1

Unit 1 **Pronouns as the Subject of a Sentence** 3

Unit 2 **Pronouns as Direct Objects** 9

Unit 3 **Pronouns as Indirect Objects** 12

Unit 4 **Pronouns in a Prepositional Phrase** 14

Unit 5 **Direct and Indirect Object Pronouns in the Same Sentence** 16

Unit 6 **Possessive Pronouns** 21

Unit 7 **Demonstrative, Indefinite, and Interrogative Pronouns** 24

Unit 8 **Numbers as Pronouns** 28

Unit 9 **The Pronoun *One*** 30

Unit 10 **Relative Pronouns** 33

Unit 11 **Reflexive Pronouns** 38

Unit 12 **Reciprocal Pronouns** 41

PART II	Prepositions	43

Unit 13 **Prepositions That Indicate Location** 45

Unit 14 **Prepositions That Indicate Movement or Direction** 50

Unit 15 **Prepositions That Indicate Time** 54

Unit 16 **Compound Prepositions** 58

Unit 17 **Prepositions That Combine with Other Words** 61

Unit 18 **Participial Prepositions** 65

Unit 19   **Postpositive Prepositions**   67

Unit 20   **Words That Require a Specific Preposition**   69

Unit 21   **Prepositions and Phrasal Verbs**   75

Unit 22   **A Variety of Prepositional Uses**   94

Appendix: Commonly Used Prepositions   97

Answer Key   99

Introduction

Pronouns

Some learners believe that they understand everything about pronouns, because they know that *pronouns replace nouns* in a sentence and because they are familiar with the personal pronouns: *I, you, he, she, it, we,* and *they.* But the story about pronouns is much longer and more complicated than that.

For one thing, there are many types of pronouns. They range from the personal pronouns that everyone identifies with relative ease to possessive pronouns, demonstrative pronouns, relative pronouns, reflexive pronouns, reciprocal pronouns, and others. The list should not frighten you. The names may seem meaningless to you now, but with some experience with the pronouns and adequate practice, they will make sense to you.

In this book you will encounter the various types of pronouns. They will be described for you, and they will be illustrated with examples. Then you will have the opportunity to practice with them in a variety of exercises.

The exercises appear in different forms in order to give you practice with the pronouns from different angles. Some of the exercises ask you to select the word that completes a sentence correctly:

> Jim had an accident with **him**/*his*/**me**/**myself** new car.

Others ask you to complete a sentence with any appropriate pronoun:

> I hit Tom, and then he hit *me* back.

And still others ask for you to write an original sentence that includes a specific target phrase:

> Target phrase: one another
> *They loved one another very much.*

The end result will be that you will have developed a better understanding of English pronouns and will have increased your effectiveness in using pronouns.

Prepositions

You probably know what each of these words mean: *to, get, out, of, my, sight.* But when the words are combined as a single phrase they become a verb with a new meaning:

New Phrase	**New Meaning**
Get out of my sight!	Leave!

The prepositions in that phrase had a lot to do with changing the meaning.

There is a rather old-fashioned rule that says that you should never end a sentence with a preposition. In general, it's not a bad rule to follow. But there are times when the rule just doesn't work. Winston Churchill, the famed Prime Minister of Great Britain and a highly competent writer and speaker, once joked about the difficulty of conforming to that rule about prepositions when he said:

> "That is nonsense up with which I shall not put."

Sometimes a preposition just has to fall at the end of a sentence in order to make sense and not to sound awkward. You will encounter prepositions here in practical forms and in forms that conform to contemporary English.

This book will guide you through the maze of prepositional types and uses and clarify their function in a sentence. They will be described and illustrated for you, and then you will have ample opportunity to practice with them in the exercises. And, as with pronouns, there will be numerous kinds of exercises for prepositions.

Take advantage of the contents of this book and increase your ability to use pronouns and prepositions effectively and accurately. This will be an important step in increasing your skill in speaking and writing English.

PRACTICE
MAKES
PERFECT

English Pronouns and Prepositions

PART I

PRONOUNS

Pronouns are almost all very small words. This fact causes some people to think that pronouns are, therefore, a small and unimportant part of the language. But the opposite is true. Understanding the various types of pronouns and how they are used is very important for developing accuracy in English.

Every pronoun shares the same simple characteristic: it is a word that replaces a noun.

Noun	Pronoun
John is young.	**He** is young.
Six men were hurt.	**Six** were hurt.
These words make no sense.	**These** make no sense.
I really enjoyed **the party**.	I really enjoyed **myself**.

You should have noticed in the list above that only the first sentence changed from a noun to a familiar pronoun form—a subject or personal pronoun. The other three pairs of examples illustrate that there is something more to pronouns than just substituting a personal pronoun for a noun.

This does not make personal pronouns unimportant. In fact, knowing how personal pronouns function in the language is a good basis for discovering how other types of pronouns function. Looking carefully at personal pronouns will be the first step toward developing an understanding of other types of pronouns and toward acquiring greater skill in using pronouns, which will make you a more effective user of English.

Pronouns as the Subject of a Sentence

The *first person* pronouns refer to one's self. The *second person* pronouns refer to others to whom you are speaking. And the *third person* pronouns are substitutes for all other nouns. The pronouns that can act as the subject of a sentence (and are for this reason called subject, or personal, pronouns) are listed in the chart below.

	Singular	**Plural**
First Person	I	we
Second Person	you	you
Third Person	he, she, it	they

Note that *you* has both a singular and plural meaning: "Mary, you are a great athlete." "Tom and Mary, you have to study more."

In addition, there are two more pronouns that are used to ask questions about people (*who*) and about things (*what*).

The pronoun *he* can replace nouns that refer to males:

the man → he

a boy → he

the doctor → he

The pronoun *she* can replace nouns that refer to females:

the woman → she

a girl → she

the doctor → she

The pronoun *it* can replace nouns that refer to objects:

the rock → it

a building → it

his nose → it

The pronoun *they* can replace nouns that refer to plurals:

> the girls → they
> men → they
> two rocks → they

The pronoun *who* can replace animate nouns to form a question:

> The man became ill. → **Who** became ill?
> A few women went shopping. → **Who** went shopping?

The pronoun *what* can replace inanimate nouns to form a question:

> Our house burned down. → **What** burned down?
> His tools are in the garage. → **What** is in the garage?

There is one notable exception to the rule that pronouns are derived by the gender of nouns. It is common to refer to a boat or sometimes an automobile as a female:

> "What a beautiful sailboat! **She's** a real beauty."
> "What about the *Titanic*?" "**She** sank in the Atlantic in 1912."
> "**She's** been a good old car, but it's time to trade her in."

Note that a noun or pronoun combined with *I* can be replaced by *we*:

> you and I = we
> she and I = we
> the boy and I = we
> the girls and I = we

The subject pronouns determine the form of the verb in the sentence. In the present tense most verbs require an *-s* ending when the subject is a third person singular pronoun or noun: *he has, the girl sings*. The other pronouns do not require an ending on the verb. The only exception to this is the verb *to be*, which has a more complicated conjugation than other verbs:

	to come	**to help**	**to be**
I	come	help	am
you	come	help	are
he, she, it	comes	helps	is
we	come	help	are
you	come	help	are
they	come	help	are

In the past tense the subject pronouns do not require an additional ending on the verb beyond the past tense formation. There is only one exception to this rule, and, again, it is the verb *to be*. Look at these examples in the past tense:

	to come	**to help**	**to be**
I	came	helped	was
you	came	helped	were
he, she, it	came	helped	was
we	came	helped	were
you	came	helped	were
they	came	helped	were

There is another second person singular pronoun. It is *thou*. It is considered archaic and is only found in very old documents or literature and in certain versions of the Bible. Its forms are:

> Subject pronoun: *thou*
> Object pronoun: *thee*
> Possessive pronouns: *thy, thine*

As the subject of a present tense sentence, *thou* requires an *-st* ending on the verb: *thou hast, thou canst*. You should be aware of this pronoun's existence, but it will not be considered further in this book.

exercise   1-1

Circle the pronoun that correctly completes each sentence.

1. **We/She/I** has to go home at five o'clock.

2. When do **you/she/he** leave on your trip?

3. **I/She/They** were frightened during the storm.

4. **I/You/We** am planning on early retirement.

5. Why are **it/you/he** crying?

6. **They/Who/We** wants to arrange a surprise party for her?

7. **He/You/We** was sound asleep.

8. **What/I/They** needs to be repaired right away?

9. Where does **I/you/she** go every afternoon?

10. **They/She/He** earn a very good salary.

exercise   1-2

Rewrite each sentence, changing the italicized noun phrase to the appropriate pronoun.

1. *My little sister* is such a sweet child.

   _____

2. *These boys* just can't seem to get along.

   _____

3. Where did *the sleepy soldiers* find a place to rest?

   _____

4. *My friends and I* spent a week camping in the mountains.

   _____

5. *The new school* burned down last night.

   _____

6. Where is *John* from?

   _____

7. *Two jet planes* roared overhead.

   _____

8. Why is *Ms. Brown* laughing?

   _____

9. Does *your arm* still hurt?

   _____

10. *Tom and I* can help you today.

   _____

You should be aware that personal pronouns used as subjects can form contractions. Contractions are formed with pronouns and certain verbs. Look at the examples that follow:

Pronoun	have	has	is	are	am	would	will
I	I've				I'm	I'd	I'll
you	you've			you're		you'd	you'll
he		he's	he's			he'd	he'll
she		she's	she's			she'd	she'll
it		it's	it's				
we	we've			we're		we'd	we'll
they	they've			they're		they'd	they'll
who		who's	who's			who'd	who'll
what		what's	what's				

There is one special contraction formed from the words *let us*: *let's*.

Other contractions are a combination of a verb and the negative word *not*:

Verb	Contraction	Verb	Contraction
are	aren't	must	mustn't
can	can't	need	needn't
could	couldn't	should	shouldn't
did	didn't	was	wasn't
do	don't	were	weren't
has	hasn't	will	won't
have	haven't	would	wouldn't
is	isn't		

Pronouns in a contraction should only be used in complete utterances and not in an elliptical phrase (a phrase in which information is understood):

> He'll arrive here on the five-thirty bus.
> I'm sure tomorrow will be a better day for you.

But it is common to respond to someone's question with an elliptical phrase. An elliptical phrase is one that leaves out certain words that are understood *from the words in the question.* In elliptical phrases contractions should *not* be used, unless the contraction is the combination of a verb and the negative word *not.* Let's look at some examples:

> Question: Is he going to work today?
> Answer: Yes, **he's** going to work today.
> Elliptical answer: Yes, **he is**. (no contraction)
>
> Question: Are you afraid of mice?
> Answer: Yes, **I'm** afraid of mice.
> Elliptical answer: Yes, **I am**. (no contraction)
>
> Question: Did she have enough money?
> Answer: No, **she didn't** have enough money.
> Elliptical answer: No, **she didn't**. (combination of a verb and *not*)

exercise 1-3

Write an elliptical answer to each of the following questions.

1. Do you like living in San Francisco?

   _____

2. Is she a good programmer?

   _____

3. Have they ever seen the Grand Canyon?

   _____

4. Was he always such a complainer?

   _____

5. Am I permitted to study in this room?

   _____

6. Aren't we spending too much time on this problem?

   _____

7. Should she really buy such an expensive car?

   _____

8. Can you understand what he's talking about?

    _____

9. Shouldn't he rest for a while?

    _____

10. Will they have to spend the night here?

    _____

Pronouns as Direct Objects

Although nouns do not change when they are used as direct objects in a sentence, most pronouns do.

Subject	Direct Object
I	me
you (singular)	you (singular)
he, she, it	him, her, it
we	us
you (plural)	you (plural)
they	them
who	whom
what	what

You should be aware that in casual language, most people substitute *who* for *whom* as the direct object form.

Now look at the pronouns when they are used as direct objects in a sentence:

Bill saw **me** at the bank yesterday.

I like **you** a lot. (singular *you*)

Mom sent **her** to the store.

We bought **it** a week ago.

She found **us** hiding in the garage.

I'll help **you**. (plural *you*)

Michael warned **them** about the danger.

Whom did you meet at the party? (or, in casual language, **Who** did you meet at the party?)

What are they making for supper?

Look at these examples that show what occurs when direct object nouns are changed to direct object pronouns:

Jim tried to kiss **the girl**. → Jim tried to kiss **her**.
They really like **their former coach**. → They really like **him**.
Who threw **the ball** to him? → Who threw **it** to him?
You'll find **the new tools** in the shed. → You'll find **them** in the shed.

---

exercise   2-1

Fill in the blank with the word or phrase shown in parentheses. Make any necessary changes to form the pronouns.

1. Why would the police want to arrest _____ (we)?

2. My uncle visited _____ (I) in Chicago.

3. Did the doctor ask _____ (you singular) about the accident?

4. John caught _____ (he) stealing a bicycle.

5. Can you join _____ (she and I) for dinner?

6. I just can't believe _____ (it)!

7. How can I reach _____ (you plural) after you move?

8. The boys watched _____ (she) all afternoon.

9. You can help _____ (Tom and I) clean up the kitchen.

10. _____ (Who) should I call about a leaky faucet?

---

exercise   2-2

Rewrite each sentence and change the direct object noun phrase to a pronoun.

1. My sister liked Jim's roommate a lot.

   _____

2. Can you understand that foreign language?

   _____

3. I bought several CDs at the mall.

   _____

4. When did you first meet my brother and me?

   _____

5. I spent a lot of money.

   _____

6. We used to visit the twins regularly.

   _____

7. I'd like to introduce my girlfriend Anita.

   _____

Pronouns as Indirect Objects

Nouns used as indirect objects look the same as when they are used as subjects or direct objects. Look at these examples with the phrase *the man*.

SUBJECT: The man is a stranger to me.

DIRECT OBJECT: Do you know the man?

INDIRECT OBJECT: I gave the man a few dollars.

But pronouns change. Pronouns used as indirect objects have the same form as pronouns used as direct objects.

Subject	Direct Object	Indirect Object
I	me	me
you (singular)	you (singular)	you (singular)
he, she, it	him, her, it	him, her, it
we	us	us
you (plural)	you (plural)	you (plural)
they	them	them
who	whom	whom
what	what	what

Notice how indirect object nouns change to pronouns:

Mike gave **the girls** the tickets. → Mike gave **them** the tickets.

I bought **James** a new shirt. → I bought **him** a new shirt.

Did Bill send **your sister** a postcard? → Did Bill send **her** a postcard?

exercise	3-1

Change the italicized indirect objects to pronouns.

1. He won't sell *Jim* the car.

2. Did you bring *your girlfriend* a gift?

_____

3. I loaned *the Smith family* a hundred dollars.

_____

4. Please give *Ms. Garcia* a copy of the will.

_____

5. I'm going to buy *the children* some new pajamas.

_____

6. James sent *his elderly aunt* a bouquet of roses.

_____

7. She wrote *her boyfriend* several letters.

_____

exercise | **3-2**

Fill in the blank with the word or phrase shown in parentheses. Make any necessary changes to form the pronouns.

1. I wanted to give _____ (you singular) something nice.

2. Please send _____ (she) a telegram with the news.

3. They brought _____ (we) breakfast in bed.

4. Can you lend _____ (I) a few dollars until tomorrow?

5. You ought to write _____ (he) a letter every week.

6. She'll buy _____ (you plural) new socks and underwear.

7. Mr. Brown gave _____ (Jim and I) a lecture on politics again.

8. I'm sending _____ (they) the directions to our new house.

9. Tell _____ (I) a story.

10. Who bought _____ (we) these tools?

Pronouns in a Prepositional Phrase

Nouns do not change their form when used in a prepositional phrase. But pronouns do, and they take the same form they do as direct or indirect objects.

Form of Pronouns That Follow Prepositions

me	us	whom
you (singular)	you (plural)	what
him, her, it	them	

In sentences, the pronouns following a preposition look like this:

Repeat this sentence **after me**.

She wants to speak **with you**. (singular)

I took a picture **of him**.

What do you know **about her**?

There's something hiding **in it**.

What do they want **from us**?

The thief was sitting **between you**. (plural)

Is that a deer coming up **to them**?

If the pronoun is *who* or *what*, the preposition often stands at the end of the question in casual speech, and *who* may be substituted for *whom*.

With whom were you chatting?

Who were you chatting **with**?

On what did you place the book?

What did you place the book **on**?

exercise	4-1

Fill in the blank with the word or phrase shown in parentheses. Make any necessary changes to form the pronouns.

1. They were asking questions about _____ (you singular).

2. I received several letters from _____ (she).

3. From _____ (who) did you borrow the money?

4. _____ (What) were they all laughing about?

5. Someone threw a rock at _____ (I).

6. This problem has nothing to do with _____ (you plural).

7. That shirt really looks good on _____ (he).

8. A crow was flying directly over _____ (they).

9. An old woman came up to _____ (we).

10. Those stories were written by _____ (the girls and I).

exercise	4-2

Fill in the blank with any preposition from the list below.

about	after	at	by	for	from
in	near	of	on	to	with

1. Three of the girls wanted to dance _____ me.

2. The artist painted a wonderful portrait _____ her.

3. _____ whom did you send the manuscript?

4. A little bird was sitting _____ it.

5. What did you put it _____?

6. I entered the building right _____ him.

7. There's a new bank _____ it.

8. The frightened dog came slowly up _____ us.

Direct and Indirect Object Pronouns in the Same Sentence

When a direct object and an indirect object are used in the same sentence and *both are nouns*, the indirect object (IO) always precedes the direct object (DO).

Father showed **Mr. Garcia** (IO) **his new car** (DO).

Will you give **the dogs** (IO) **some water** (DO)?

If only the indirect object is changed to a pronoun, the same word order occurs:

Father showed **him** (IO) **his new car** (DO).

Will you give **them** (IO) **some water** (DO)?

But if the direct object is changed to a pronoun, there is a significant change in the word order and the indirect object becomes the object of the preposition *to* or *for*. This occurs whether the indirect object is a noun or a pronoun. Look at these examples:

Direct Object as Noun	Direct Object as Pronoun
I sent the men **some fresh coffee**.	I sent **it** *to the men*.
Who gave him **these gifts**?	Who gave **them** *to him*?
We bought the girls **a few flowers**.	We bought **them** *for the girls*.
Bring me **a hammer**.	Bring **it** *to me*.

exercise   5-1

Rewrite each sentence changing the direct object to a pronoun.

1. The magician showed us a fantastic trick.

   _____

2. Don't give the children the cookies.

   _____

3. I can't lend you the money.

   _____

4. Who sent your cousin this awful letter?

   _____

5. Tom is going to buy them a kitten.

   _____

6. The lawyer did him a favor.

   _____

7. The lonely soldier wrote his girlfriend four long letters.

   _____

8. She gave me her phone number.

   _____

9. Uncle Robert bought us a new TV.

   _____

10. Do you send them a check every week?

    _____

exercise   5-2

Rewrite each sentence, changing the direct and indirect objects to pronouns.

1. The judge sent the lawyers the documents.

   _____

2. Why did you show Mary that picture?

   _____

3. I can't lend my boyfriend so much money.

    _____

4. Dr. Brown gave the nurse the surgical instruments.

    _____

5. Show the police officer your license.

    _____

6. They're going to buy their nephew several CDs.

    _____

7. Will you save Maria a seat at this table?

    _____

exercise   5-3

Rewrite each sentence, changing the italicized word or phrase to a pronoun. Make all other necessary changes.

1. *Several boys* were standing on the corner and laughing.

    _____

2. Someone threw *a rock* through that window!

    _____

3. Bill wants to buy his mother *a birthday present.*

    _____

4. You shouldn't speak about *your brother* in that terrible way.

    _____

5. Where did you buy *such a beautiful necklace?*

    _____

6. Ms. Smith has moved out of *her apartment.*

    _____

7. Do you know *these women?*

    _____

8. *Bill and I* were on our way to the party when it happened.

    _____

9. I bought you *some flowers.*

_____

10. Do you want to go there with *my sister and me?*

_____

11. *That young lady* has been elected chairperson of the committee.

_____

12. He hates *spiders.*

_____

13. Put *those old clothes* in the attic, please.

_____

14. Is *that tall man* the new boss?

_____

15. We love *beautiful warm weather.*

_____

exercise   5-4

Write three original sentences with the pronoun given in parentheses. In the first sentence, use the pronoun as a direct object. In the second sentence, use the pronoun as an indirect object. In the third sentence, use the pronoun as the object of a preposition.

1. (I) _____

_____

_____

2. (she) _____

_____

_____

3. (we) _____

_____

_____

4.(they) _____

_____

_____

5.(who) _____

_____

_____

A Word of Caution

You will sometimes hear native speakers use pronouns incorrectly. This is particularly true when two pronouns are used together or a noun and a pronoun are used together—for example, *you and I, Tom and he.*

You have seen examples in this book that show which pronouns are used as the subject of a sentence. But compare what is correct with what you might hear a native say:

Correct: Tom and **she** are playing baseball tomorrow.

Incorrect: Tom and **her** are playing baseball tomorrow.

Correct: **He** and **I** have the same birthday.

Incorrect: **Him** and **me** have the same birthday.

Similar errors occur when such phrases are used as a direct or indirect object or the object of a preposition. In order to sound loftier, some speakers "overcorrect" the pronoun and use a nominative case pronoun where an objective case pronoun is really required. This seems most prevalent with the first person singular pronoun *I*:

Correct: Martha gave Barbara and **me** a list of chores.

Incorrect: Martha gave Barbara and **I** a list of chores.

Correct: Did he want to speak with both you and **me**?

Incorrect: Did he want to speak with both you and **I**?

Possessive Pronouns

Just as nouns can be formed to show ownership or possession, so too can pronouns. Most nouns add an apostrophe plus an -s to show possession: *John's car, the woman's dress, a winter's night.* But pronouns form a completely new word. The following chart shows each subject pronoun and its possessive form.

Subject Pronoun	Possessive Pronoun 1	Possessive Pronoun 2
I	my	mine
you (singular)	your	yours
he, she, it	his, her, its	his, her, its
we	our	ours
you (plural)	your	yours
they	their	theirs
who	whose	whose

A possessive pronoun 1 is used to modify a noun. It is always used in a combination of the possessive pronoun and a noun or noun phrase. It shows to whom something belongs:

I have books. = my books

You have a car. = your car

We have money. = our money

Who has a funny hat? = whose funny hat

The third person possessive pronouns are used to replace possessive nouns:

the young man's wallet = his wallet

our daughter's party = her party

the roach's nest = its nest

my friends' new house = their new house

There is a difference in the use of the possessive pronoun 1 and 2. The possessive pronoun 2 *replaces a possessive pronoun 1 and a noun* when the noun is understood.

> This is **my glove**. = This is **mine**.
> Where is **your car**? = Where is **yours**?
> That was **his dinner**. = That was **his**.
> **Her dog** is smarter. = **Hers** is smarter.
> Did you meet **our friends**? = Did you meet **ours**?
> **Their son** is a sailor. = **Theirs** is a sailor.

exercise   6-1

Rewrite each sentence changing the possessive noun phrase to a possessive pronoun.

1. The pretty girl's brother goes to college.

   _____

2. Do you know Mr. Brown's niece?

   Yes, I know his niece.

3. The snake's hole was behind a large rock.

   _____

4. The birds' chirping woke me up early.

   Their chirping

5. She loved the ballerina's solo.

   _____

6. I had to hold my mother's purse.

   I had to hold her purse.

7. The old sow's piglets slept in a cool pile of mud.

   _____

8. Did you borrow your sister's skis?

   Did you borrow her skis.

9. The strikers' demands were too much for the company.

   _____

10. Where is the little puppies' bed going to be?

    Where is the their bed going to be.

exercise   6-2

Fill in the blank with the possessive pronoun formed from the one in parentheses.

1. I wanted to dance with _____ (she) older sister.

2. Will you help me carry ____*my*____ (I) books up to the second floor?

3. They said ____*Your*____ (you) father had been a colonel in the army.

4. ____*Our*____ (We) tent was put up near a bend in the river.

5. Michael wanted to spend time at ____*Our*____ (Maria and I) campsite.

6. I still haven't met _____ (they) parents.

7. _____ (Who) sailboat is that out on the lake?

8. I just can't get interested in _____ (he) novels.

9. _____ (It) roof has been replaced with cedar shingles.

10. Ms. Garcia wanted to borrow _____ (you and I) garden hose.

Demonstrative, Indefinite, and Interrogative Pronouns

Demonstrative Pronouns

It is easy to identify a demonstrative pronoun. It is a pronoun that points out the noun that is being spoken or written about. It modifies the noun like an adjective. The four demonstrative pronouns are *this*, *that*, *these*, and *those*.

This and *these* indicate something that is close by. *This* is used with singular nouns, and *these* is used with plural nouns:

This man is a good friend of mine. (The man is here.)

These books are on sale now. (The books are here.)

That and *those* indicate something that is far away. *That* is used with singular nouns, and *those* is used with plural nouns:

That woman is my teacher. (I see the woman in the distance.)

Did you see **those** airplanes? (Did you see the airplanes in the distance?)

exercise 7-1

Using the information in parentheses, fill in the blank with the appropriate demonstrative pronoun.

1. (located next to me) I found _____ puppy behind a bush.

2. (on my lap) She thought _____ magazines were interesting.

3. (two blocks from here) _____ tall building is the city hall.

4. (in my hand) Would you like some of _____ nuts?

5. (above the city) _____ dark clouds mean a storm is coming.

6. (in another state) _____ town is about two hundred miles from here.

7. (in the apartment down the hall) Why do _____ people make so much noise?

8. (around my neck) I bought _____ necklace on sale.

9. (out in the yard) _____ swing set is just for children.

10. (back at the school) _____ boys played soccer all afternoon.

Indefinite Pronouns

The indefinite pronouns are used to refer to a person or thing that has been mentioned earlier. Their list is rather long:

all	either	neither	several
another	everybody	no one	some
any	everyone	nobody	somebody
anybody	everything	none	someone
anyone	few	nothing	something
anything	many	one	
both	most	other	
each	much	others	

Like any other pronoun, an indefinite pronoun replaces a noun, but it is usually a noun that has appeared earlier in an utterance. Look at these examples:

> **The children** were in an accident. But **all** are safe and sound now.
> Were **the robbers** finally caught? Only **some** of them.
> **Mary and Barbara** were born on the same day. Yes, but **each** has a separate birthday party.

You need to be aware that a few of the indefinite pronouns can be used as a singular or plural: *all, any, more, most, none,* and *some.* Here are a few examples:

Singular
All is well.
Most was done by John.
Some was left on the table.

Plural
All speak English and Spanish.
Most aren't going to vote for him.
Some think she's very beautiful.

| exercise | 7-2 |

Circle the indefinite pronoun that best completes each sentence.

1. He has three brothers. **Some/Much/Each** served in the navy for three years.

2. I bought seven tickets. **All/Something/Neither** were purchased at a discount.

3. The children didn't like her, and **most/none/any** would play with her.

4. **Nobody/Other/Either** put in enough time on the project.

5. **Someone/Many/Everything** he said turned out to be a lie.

6. Many of them enjoyed the concert. **Others/Each/Another** went home early.

7. They invited a hundred guests. **Much/Several/Anybody** are already in the reception hall.

8. The two girls took part in the competition, but **any/somebody/neither** had a chance of winning.

9. **Anyone/Another/Few** found without proper identification will be arrested.

10. **Many/Anything/Much** has been said about the problem, but nothing has been done.

Interrogative Pronouns

The interrogative pronouns are *who, whom, whose, which,* and *what.* They are called *interrogative* because they ask a question. And like other pronouns, they replace nouns.

> **Who** invited these people to the party? (**Tom** invited these people.)
> **Whom** can I rely upon in these difficult times? (I can rely upon **Tom**.)
> **Whose** was voted the best cake at the fair? (**Tom's** cake was voted best.)
> **Which** is the hat you decided to buy? (I decided to buy that **gray** hat.)
> **What** is he talking about? (He is talking about **the theory of relativity**.)

These pronouns can be separated into *nominative, objective,* and *possessive* forms:

Nominative	Objective	Possessive
who	whom	whose
which	which	
what	what	

The nominative is used as the subject of a sentence. The objective is used as the direct object, indirect object, or object of a preposition. The possessive form shows ownership. Look at these examples with *who* and *which*:

> Nominative: **Who** rented your apartment?
> Objective: **Whom** will they elect as president?
> Possessive: **Whose** is the brightest child?

Nominative: **Which** came first, the chicken or the egg?
Objective: **Which** do you want to sell?

Just like indefinite pronouns, interrogative pronouns are used when the noun in question is understood.

exercise   **7-3**

Change the italicized word or phrase to the appropriate interrogative pronoun and form a question.

1. *This gentleman* would like to order some dinner.

   _____

2. She found *some old documents* in the drawer.

   _____

3. *Mr. Brown's* is the fastest horse in the race.

   _____

4. They were discussing *the last one.*

   _____

5. Several women were talking about *the coming election.*

   _____

6. We met *him* while traveling in Mexico.

   _____

7. *Maria and James* spent a lot of time in the mountains.

   _____

8. They prefer *the new one.*

   _____

9. *A long, black snake* slithered across the road.

   _____

10. They received several letters *from their attorney.*

    _____

Numbers as Pronouns

If a pronoun is a word that replaces a noun, then *a number* that does the same thing can be considered a pronoun. If the number stands alone, it is no longer just a numerical value or an adjective modifying a noun. It functions as a pronoun. Look at some examples:

Number Modifying a Noun	Number Used as a Pronoun
One boy was crying.	**One** felt sad but would not cry.
Three kittens played with the ball.	**Three** were born just a few minutes apart.
Ten soldiers watched the enemy approach.	**Ten** fled the battlefield in fear.

Just like indefinite pronouns, numbers are used as pronouns when the noun in question is understood.

Numbers as Nouns

Careful! A number can also act as a noun. When it is a noun, the verb used is singular. When it is a pronoun, the verb is plural (except with *one*):

Noun: **Thirteen** is an unlucky number.

Pronoun: **Thirteen** are hiding in the brush.

Noun: **One** is pronounced like the word *won*.

Pronoun: **One** is still in the nest.

exercise   8-1

Rewrite each sentence changing the noun phrase to a number used as a pronoun.

1. Five little boys were playing in the mud.

   Five were playing in the mud.

2. I have eleven pairs of socks in that drawer.

   I have eleven in that drawer

3. The two older gentlemen are friends of mine.

   The two are friends of mine.

4. One excellent suggestion came from Ms. Garcia.

   One came from Ms. Garcia

5. There were five clean plates on the table a moment ago.

   There were five on the table a moment ago.

6. The new sales clerk sold her eight beautiful skirts.

   The new sales clerk sold her eight

7. Three people applied for the same job.

   Three applied for the same job.

8. There were at least fifty pennies scattered about the floor.

   There were at least fifty scattered about the floor.

The Pronoun *One*

Many people use the pronoun *one* in a more traditional or formal style. But it can be replaced by *you* in casual speech. Either pronoun—*one* or *you*—is used when someone does not want to use a pronoun that identifies a specific person; they are used to speak *in general*. If you substitute the pronoun *someone* for *one*, you will have the approximate meaning of *one*. Like other pronouns, *one* and *you* have four functions:

Nominative	Objective	Possessive	Reflexive
one	one	one's	oneself
you	you	your	yourself

(The reflexive will be taken up separately in Unit 11.)

Look how they are used in sentences:

> FORMAL: If **one** believes in ghosts, **one** might be considered superstitious.

> APPROXIMATE MEANING: If **someone** believes in ghosts, **someone** might be considered superstitious.

> CASUAL: If **you** believe in ghosts, **you** might be considered superstitious.

One is a third person pronoun and, therefore, verbs used with this pronoun require the same ending as any other third person pronoun: *he talks, one talks*; *she goes, one goes*; *it is, one is*. But if *you* replaces *one*, the ending *-s* is not required in the present tense.

> FORMAL: If **one plays** fairly, **one** always **wins**.

> CASUAL: If **you play** fairly, **you** always **win**.

Do not confuse this special use of *you* with the second person pronoun *you*. They can be used in identical sentences, but the meaning of each sentence is different.

Second person pronoun: John, **you** should always wash your hands.
Replacement for third person pronoun *one*: **You** should always wash your hands. (One should always wash one's hands. Someone should always wash his hands.)

exercise 9-1

Rewrite each sentence changing the pronoun one *in each sentence to* you.

1. One must have strength to carry on.

   _____

2. Should one always be on time for one's lessons?

   _____

3. If one loses one's wallet, one should report that to the police.

   _____

4. One ought to try to stay in shape.

   _____

5. When one drinks too much, one gets drunk.

   _____

6. One has little choice when it comes to love.

   _____

7. One should always behave oneself.

   _____

8. How can one be so mean to her?

   _____

9. If one has too much time on one's hands, one needs to find a job.

   _____

10. When one has humility, one also has respect.

   _____

exercise	9-2

Rewrite each sentence below twice: once with the pronoun one *and once with the casual replacement pronoun* you.

1. She might get into a lot of trouble.

   _____

   _____

2. If they speak slowly, they are better understood.

   _____

   _____

3. My friends ought to consider taking the train there.

   _____

   _____

4. Should he criticize his own mistakes?

   _____

   _____

5. Children learn slowly when they are very young.

   _____

   _____

6. In time, people accept their limitations.

   _____

   _____

7. If the man carries on like a fool, he'll be considered a fool.

   _____

   _____

8. When the girls get a little too heavy, they should begin to exercise.

   _____

   _____

Relative Pronouns

Two sentences can be combined by using a relative pronoun. If the same noun appears in two sentences, one of the nouns can be changed to a relative pronoun and the two sentences can be stated as one, the one with the relative pronoun being called a *relative clause*.

> He likes the car. His father bought the car. = He likes the car *that* **his father bought**.

The English relative pronouns are:

who, whom, whose → used to replace animate nouns

which → used to replace inanimate nouns

that → used to replace animate or inanimate nouns

In casual speech *whom* is almost always replaced by *who*.

There is also an *elliptical* relative pronoun form, which omits the use of a relative pronoun entirely.

> RELATIVE PRONOUN *THAT*: He likes the car **that** his father bought.

> ELLIPTICAL FORM: He likes the car his father bought.

Although there are some traditional rules for choosing between *that* and the forms of *who* and *which*, in casual speech they are often used interchangeably:

> This is the man **that** I told you about.

> This is the man **who** I told you about.

The general rule for more formal usage requires using *that* if the relative clause is *restrictive*. A restrictive relative clause is one that defines or identifies the antecedent (the word to which the relative pronoun refers). Look at this example:

> The house **that his grandfather built many years ago** burned down last night.

The relative clause (in bold type) identifies *which house* burned down last night. The sentence would not have the same meaning if the relative clause were omitted. The meaning of *house* is restricted by the information provided in the relative clause.

The relative pronouns *who* and *which* tend to be used in relative clauses that provide nonessential information. Nonrestrictive clauses are set off by commas. The meaning of the original sentence is not affected by such relative clauses:

> Our mayor, **who has been in office for two years**, is traveling to Canada.
> Some articles, **which appeared in newspapers across the country**, ridiculed the mayor.

In these nonrestrictive relative clauses, the *mayor* and the *articles* are not identified by the relative clauses. They do not answer the questions, *Which mayor? Which articles?* The sentences make complete sense when the relative clauses are omitted:

> Our mayor is traveling to Canada.
> Some articles ridiculed the mayor.

When changing a noun to a relative pronoun, the function of the noun must remain the function of the relative pronoun: subject, direct object, indirect object, object of a preposition, or possessive. Here are some examples that use the sentence, *The boxer was the champ*:

> Subject: The boxer won the bout. → The boxer **that** won the bout was the champ.
> Direct object: He knocked out the boxer. → The boxer **that** he knocked out was the champ.
> Object of preposition: I spoke with the boxer. → The boxer **that** I spoke **with** was the champ.
> Possession: The boxer's training was best. → The boxer **whose** training was best was the champ.

If a noun is used as an indirect object, the relative pronoun becomes the object of the preposition *to* or *for* in the relative clause:

> Indirect object: I gave the boxer some good advice. → The boxer **that** I gave some good advice **to** was the champ.

When the relative pronoun is *that* and is the object of a preposition, the preposition must stand at the end of the clause:

> We found the scientist **that** Professor Jones had written **about**.

If the relative pronoun is *who(m)* or *which*, the preposition will stand before the relative pronoun in formal style but at the end of the clause in more casual style. Notice again that nonrestrictive relative clauses are separated by commas:

> Formal: It was a terrible event, **about which** much had been written.
> Casual: It was a terrible event, **which** much had been written **about**.

> Formal: The criminal, **from whom** they received several threats, was finally located.
> Casual: The criminal, **who** they received several threats **from**, was finally located.

Use *whose* for the possessive of an animate. Use *of which* or *whose* for the possessive of an inanimate:

They visited their grandfather, **whose** farm is located in Maryland.
She bought a dreadful hat, the color **of which** was green.
She bought a dreadful hat, **whose** color was green.

The elliptical form of a relative clause occurs when the relative pronoun is a direct object or the object of a preposition. Look at these examples:

Direct object: They spoke with the thief **that** the police arrested yesterday.
Elliptical form: They spoke with the thief the police arrested yesterday.

Object of preposition: I found the document **that** you inquired **about**.
Elliptical form: I found the document you inquired **about**.

In the elliptical form of a relative pronoun used as the object of a preposition, the preposition is always at the end of the clause.

exercise	10-1

Combine the pairs of sentences below with the relative pronoun that *or* whose. *Make any necessary changes.*

1. He found a puppy. The puppy needed a home.

   _____

2. Where did you put the groceries? I bought the groceries at the supermarket.

   _____

3. That's my car. My car has the convertible top.

   _____

4. There's the scientist. I told you about the scientist.

   _____

5. Do you know the woman? The woman's son is serving in the army.

   _____

6. They hired the lawyer. They got the best deal from the lawyer.

   _____

7. I need the map. The map has Cook County on it.

   _____

8. I was introduced to the girl. John was dancing with the girl.

   _____

9. Don't spend the money. I put the money on the dresser.

   _____

10. Do you know the song? I'm playing the song on the piano.

   _____

exercise   10-2

Rewrite the sentences that can be changed to the elliptical form. Be careful. Not all can be changed.

1. I lost the book that I got from Maria last week.

   _____

2. We like the dress, which was probably designed in Paris.

   _____

3. He read a sentence, which he can't understand at all.

   _____

4. I have all the documents that I was speaking of.

   _____

5. Will you give me some money, which I can use to buy new underwear?

   _____

6. The champion, who is a native of Mexico, is touring the United States.

   _____

7. He bought a used car that had been in an accident.

   _____

8. Maria wants to use the umbrella that Mom bought last week.

   _____

9. Do you understand the words that I wrote on this sheet of paper?

   _____

10. I like Uncle Henry, from whom I received a beautiful gift.

   _____

exercise   10-3

Complete each sentence with any appropriate relative clause.

1. Please show me the books _____ .

2. I met the actor _____ .

3. He bought a watch that _____ .

4. The boss, who _____ , is rather nice.

5. Where are the gifts _____ ?

6. This car, which _____ , is from Germany.

7. I have the DVD _____ .

Reflexive Pronouns

The personal pronouns have a form that is used when that form is in the objective case and is the *counterpart* of its personal pronoun. That form is called a *reflexive pronoun*. The reflexive pronouns look like this:

Subject Pronoun	Object Pronoun	Reflexive Pronoun
I	me	myself
you (singular)	you	yourself
he	him	himself
she	her	herself
it	it	itself
we	us	ourselves
you (plural)	you	yourselves
they	them	themselves
one	one	oneself

If the subject pronoun and the object pronoun refer to the same person, you should use the reflexive pronoun counterpart in the sentence. If the object pronoun refers to someone or something else, use its object pronoun form:

I suddenly saw **myself** in the mirror. (counterpart of *I*)

I suddenly saw **him** in the mirror. (different person)

We sometimes have to help **ourselves**. (counterpart of *we*)

We sometimes have to help **them**. (different persons)

Notice the difference between these pairs of sentences and the use of *him* and *himself*:

USING NOUNS: **Jim** accidentally hurt **Jim**.

USING PRONOUNS: **Jim** accidentally hurt **himself**.

USING NOUNS: **Jim** accidentally hurt **Michael**.

USING PRONOUNS: **Jim** accidentally hurt **him**.

exercise	11-1

Rewrite each sentence, changing the italicized word or phrase to the appropriate reflexive pronoun.

1. She sometimes writes stories about *her friends*.

   _____

2. We really enjoyed *the party* very much.

   _____

3. My uncle cut *his little finger* with a sharp knife.

   _____

4. The ugly dragon hid *the bones* behind a pile of stones.

   _____

5. I described *the boys* honestly.

   _____

6. Would you recommend *this woman* for the job?

   _____

7. The girls saw *their reflection* in the still water of the pond.

   _____

8. He didn't recognize *the gentleman* in his new suit of clothes.

   _____

9. A young woman was admiring *the dress* in the store window.

   _____

10. Maria and Juan! You've hurt *him* again! Shame on you!

   _____

exercise	11-2

Rewrite the following sentences with each of the pronouns given in parentheses. Use the appropriate reflexive pronouns.

1. John believes himself to be innocent.

   a. (we) _____

   b. (I) _____

c. (she) _____

d. (you plural) _____

2. She considers herself lucky.

a. (they) _____

b. (I) _____

c. (you singular) _____

d. (he) _____

Reciprocal Pronouns

There are only two reciprocal pronouns: *each other* and *one another*. They are never used as the subject of a sentence, and they always refer to a plural antecedent. Their use is similar to how a reflexive pronoun is used, but they refer back to two or more persons or things in a plural antecedent. Look at these examples:

Maria helps Tom. Tom helps Maria. → Maria and Tom help **one another**.

or Maria and Tom help **each other**.

He loves her. She loves him. → They love **one another**.
or They love **each other**.

Two boys spoke with five girls. → They spoke with **one another**.
or They spoke with **each other**.

You saw my lesson. I saw your lesson. → You and I saw **one another's** lesson.
or You and I saw **each other's** lesson.

Notice how a possessive pronoun is changed to a possessive formed with an *apostrophe -s: my* lesson, *your* lesson = *one another's* lesson.

exercise 12-1

Rewrite each of the pairs of sentences as one sentence using a reciprocal pronoun.

1. My father sits next to my mother. My mother sits next to my father.

   _____

2. The soprano harmonizes with the tenor. The tenor harmonizes with the soprano.

   _____

3. The boys danced with the girls. The girls danced with the boys.

_____

4. My boss spoke about the manager. The manager spoke about my boss.

_____

5. St. Paul is located near Minneapolis. Minneapolis is located near St. Paul.

_____

6. Barbara kissed Juan. Juan kissed Barbara.

_____

7. The lioness slept near the three cubs. The three cubs slept near the lioness.

_____

8. You respect me. I respect you.

_____

9. James sang for Maria. Maria sang for James.

_____

10. He likes her voice. She likes his voice.

_____

exercise   12-2

Write three original sentences using the reciprocal pronouns in parentheses.

1. (one another)

a. _____

b. _____

c. _____

2. (each other)

a. _____

b. _____

c. _____

PART II

PREPOSITIONS

Prepositions are another category of words that, like pronouns, are sometimes underestimated. Prepositions are not simply little words that introduce a prepositional phrase such as *in the room, from the top floor, near the beach,* or *with mother.* Many prepositions have some very specific uses. Sometimes they even act as other parts of speech. They can be adverbs. Or they can be the prefix on a noun or verb. And they can combine with other words to create a completely new meaning, far different from the original meaning of the individual words.

Prepositions show the relationship between a noun or a pronoun and some other element in a sentence or phrase. Although numerous prepositions can be used in the same position in a sentence, the simple change of a preposition makes a significant change in the meaning of the sentence. Prepositions may look like insignificant little words, but in reality they have very important functions, and the effective user of English has to understand those functions.

The variety of prepositions is not great. But there are clearly defined differences between the categories of prepositions. An examination of these categories is a good place to start.

Prepositions That Indicate Location

Location can be thought of as the *area, point,* or *surface* of something. Certain prepositions indicate those locations. Here are some of the most commonly used ones:

above	in back of
along	in front of
among	in the middle of
at	near
behind	next to
below	on
beside	over
between	under
in	with

Most of these prepositions make sense in the same sentence, because they all indicate location:

The boy is **at** the table.

The boy is **behind** the table.

The boy is **beside** the table.

The boy is **next to** the table.

The boy is **under** the table.

Besides the verb *to be,* which is frequently used to show location, there are several other verbs that also indicate *where* someone or something is:

to be found	to remain
to be located	to sit
to be situated	to stand
to lie	to stay
to live	

Of course, there are many other such verbs. Those in the preceding list are among the ones used frequently. Look at these examples:

Is Guadalajara located **in** the east or west?
The center of the earthquake was situated **near** Los Angeles.
Shells like this can be found **along** the banks of the river.
John sits **in front of** me.
The girl was lying **on** a cot and resting.
A stranger stood **next to** us.
I have to remain **at** my workbench until noon.
You can stay **with** me.
We live **between** two large houses.

As long as you know the meaning of the prepositions, you can use them with relative accuracy. But in English, just like in all other languages, certain prepositions can only be used with certain verbs or phrases. And even if two or more prepositions can be used with the same phrase, there is a change in meaning—even if it's only a slight change.

Let's look at the prepositions *at* and *in*. They are used quite commonly and have a meaning that is easy to understand. In most cases, *at* is used to show that someone or something is positioned next to a horizontal or vertical surface:

at the table	at the door
at the computer	at the window
at the desk	at the blackboard

The preposition *in* indicates that someone or something is located *inside* something:

in the car	in the city
in the house	in the box
in the garden	in the center

These two prepositions, while having very distinct uses in a sentence, are also often used with the same phrases. But when they are, the meanings are different.

Use *at* to show that someone is *at* the location of his or her occupation, preoccupation, or some activity:

at school	at the store	at the hospital
at the movies	at the library	at the factory

With certain phrases, *in* can also be used:

in school	in the store	in the hospital
in the movies	in the library	in the factory

Notice the difference in meaning between the two prepositions:

at school = Someone is on the campus of the school, perhaps inside the building, or perhaps outside the building. This person is probably a student or teacher: "The chemistry teacher was **at school** until 7:00 P.M."

in school = Someone is inside the school building. This person is probably a student or teacher: "The injured student was **in school** again today."

Take note of yet another difference of meaning when the definite article *the* is added to the phrase:

at **the** school = Someone is on the campus of the school, perhaps inside the building, or perhaps outside the building. This person is *not necessarily* a student or teacher: "The landscaper was **at the school** to plant some new shrubs."

in **the** school = Someone is inside the school building. This person is *not necessarily* a student or teacher: "My father was **in the school** for a meeting."

There are several phrases that omit the definite article *the* when the preposition *at* is involved. Such phrases indicate that someone is *involved in the activity* described in the phrase:

He's **at work**. = He is working.
They're **at church**. = They're attending a religious ceremony.
The children are **at play**. = The children are playing.
She's **at home**. = She is staying in her house.
Tom's **at lunch**. = Tom is eating lunch. (also used with *breakfast, dinner*, and *supper*)
He's **at class**. = He is attending a class.

In general, *at* indicates that someone is involved in an activity at a location. *In* says that someone is inside that location:

The students are **at** school. (They are on campus somewhere.)
The students are **in** school. (They are in the building in their classes.)

Father is **at** the hospital. (Father is visiting. Or he may be a doctor or nurse.)
Father is **in** the hospital. (Father is a patient. Or he was outside. Now he's inside.)

Maria is **at** the factory. (She probably works there.)
Maria is **in** the factory. (She was outside. Now she's inside.)

Mom is **at** the store. (She is shopping there. Or perhaps she works there.)
Mom is **in** the store. (She was outside. Now she's inside.)

Be sure to distinguish between the prepositions *among* and *between*. Use *among* to say that you are in the company of more than just two people. Use *between* to say that you are in the company of only two people:

He sat **among** the members of the tribe and told them stories.
My sister sat **between** Jim and me.

Another pair of prepositions is often used to show "by means of what transportation" a person travels. It is common to use the preposition *by* to show the concept of traveling in a conveyance: *I went by car. We travel by plane. They go by train.* But *in* and *on* are also often used to show location on the forms of transportation:

We were **in the car** ready to leave for vacation.
They're **on a train** somewhere in Oregon.
What **bus** were you **on**?
Haven't you ever been **on a plane** before?

exercise   13-1

Select the preposition that best completes each sentence.

1. A tiny rabbit was hiding **under/with/on** a bush.

2. Please don't sit **at/next to/over** me.

3. We saw several baby birds **at/behind/in** a nest in that tree.

4. There was nothing **below/with/among** the plane but empty space.

5. Father stays **on/above/at** the factory until 5:00 P.M.

6. An angry man stood directly **with/in the middle of/at** us.

7. John stayed **between/beside/among** me the entire time.

8. I saw Maria **in back of/above/among** the many people at the party.

9. There was a huge bug sitting **on/with/at** my bed!

10. I saw a stranger crouching **above/between/at** my car and the truck.

exercise   13-2

Fill in the blank with any appropriate word or phrase.

1. I saw a jet flying above _____.

2. Someone was hiding under _____.

3. Are you familiar with _____?

4. My sisters both work at _____.

5. The frightened kitten hid in _____.

6. Someone stood behind _____.

7. Who was sitting among _____?

8. There's nothing in front of _____.

9. Gray clouds hovered over _____.

10. Have a seat next to _____.

11. He found his keys on _____.

12. I found a couple seats beside _____.

13. Let's set up our camp near _____.

14. We used to live between _____.

15. A puppy sat lazily in the middle of _____.

exercise	13-3

Write original sentences with the prepositional phrases given in parentheses. Use the prepositional phrase to show a location.

1. (on the train) _____

2. (at work) _____

3. (behind the dresser) _____

4. (next to her) _____

5. (in the hospital) _____

6. (with Maria) _____

7. (between them) _____

8. (over the mountains) _____

9. (in front of us) _____

10. (under a palm tree) _____

Prepositions That Indicate Movement or Direction

The prepositions in this category do not suggest where someone or something is located. Instead, they describe someone's or something's movement or direction. Below is a list of some commonly used prepositions for this concept:

along	off
at	on
by	onto
from	out of
in	to
into	toward(s)

There are two forms of this preposition: *toward* and *towards*. Both are acceptable.

Certain verbs tell you that a preposition is being used to show location: *to be, to be located, to sit,* and many more. Certain other verbs tell you that a preposition is being used to show movement or direction. Here are some important ones:

to come	to journey
to drive	to jump
to fall	to return
to fly	to run
to go	to travel
to hurry	to walk

Just like prepositions that show location, a variety of prepositions that show movement or direction can be used in the same sentence. The basic sentence remains the same, but the preposition alters the kind of movement or direction involved. Look at these example sentences:

> The women walked **along** the river.
> The women walked **from** the river.
> The women walked **into** the river.
> The women walked **out of** the river.
> The women walked **to** the river.
> The women walked **toward** the river.

You need to be aware of the difference between *to* and *toward*. The preposition *to* says that someone *is going in the direction of a place and will arrive there soon*:

> John is going **to** the park.

The preposition *toward* means that someone is going in the direction of a place but may decide to change direction:

> John is going **toward** the park. (But he may decide to turn left and go to the bank instead.)

The prepositions *in* and *on* are used to show location. But they are also used to show movement or direction. Traditionally, only *into* and *onto* are used to show movement or direction, but many people today use *in* and *on* in place of them:

> She runs **into** the house.   She runs **in** the house.
> He fell **onto** the floor.   He fell **on** the floor.

If you consider the phrase *She runs in the house* literally, it means that *a girl is inside a house and running*. But English speakers know what is meant by this sentence from the context of the conversation where that sentence was used. So in casual speech you will hear both *in* and *into* and *on* and *onto* used interchangeably.

exercise 14-1

Select the preposition that best completes each sentence.

1. The children ran **in/toward/at** the gate.

2. The young couple strolled **along/out of/into** the beach.

3. The ball rolled **off/in/at** the table.

4. Is Thomas already **at/to/in** work?

5. I was hurrying **at/to/in** my desk.

6. Someone came running **into/onto/off** the room.

7. We slowly drove **off/at/by** their house.

8. Ms. Brown came **from/toward/at** England last year.

9. The poor girl fell **out of/onto/by** bed.

10. I dropped the tools **into/from/off** the box.

Fill in the blank with any appropriate word or phrase.

1. The cattle were heading toward _____.

2. Someone came out of _____.

3. Why were you going into _____?

4. My family frequently travels to _____.

5. Do you come from _____?

6. The carpenter fell off _____.

7. The burglar quietly climbed onto _____.

8. Maria wants to come into _____.

9. The men were walking along _____.

10. He came at _____ with a knife.

11. She drove by _____ without stopping.

12. What time did you come home from _____?

13. We're planning on traveling to _____.

14. The cat jumped into _____.

15. The woman moved cautiously toward _____.

Write original sentences with the prepositional phrases given in parentheses. Use the prepositional phrase to show movement or direction.

1. (along the shore) _____

2. (by the school) _____

3. (from the yard) _____

4. (into the living room) _____

5. (onto the shelf) _____

6. (off the bed) _____

7. (out of the garage) _____

8. (to the mountains) _____

9. (toward the wall) _____

10. (into a darkened room) _____

Prepositions That Indicate Time

There are several prepositions that are used in expressions of time:

after	from
at	in
before	on
by	since
during	to
for	until

These prepositions are used with a variety of moments in time and in phrases that answer the question *when*. Some, such as *at, on, in* and *for*, have a limited use.

The preposition *at* is used primarily to point out an event in time or a time shown on a clock:

> **at** dawn, **at** dusk, **at** daybreak, **at** holiday time, **at** lunchtime, **at** midnight, **at** the end of the day, **at** 4:30 P.M., **at** 11:55 A.M.

> The soldiers finally got back **at** dawn.

On is used primarily with days of the week and dates:

> **on** Monday, **on** Tuesday, **on** Wednesday, **on** Thursday, **on** Friday, **on** Saturday, **on** Sunday, **on** June twelfth, **on** the fifteenth of May

> We're starting a new project **on** the first of the month.

Use *in* for a nonspecific time of a day, of a month, of a year, or of a season:

> **in** the morning, **in** January, **in** 2001, **in** summer

> We like going camping **in** autumn.

Use *for* with a specific event in time:

> **for** Christmas, **for** the holidays, **for** your birthday party, **for** the celebration
> I'll be there **for** your baby's christening.

Most other prepositions can be used in many varied expressions of time:

> She can be here **by** five o'clock.
> I want to speak with you **before** the end of the day.
> He works every day **from** dawn **to** dusk.
> The drought has continued **since** last June.
> We spend a lot of time in Mexico **during** the winter months.
> Tom won't come home **until** next year.
> Maria went out to dinner **after** work yesterday.

From and *to* are usually used in the same sentence to show a long period of time. *Until* often replaces *to*:

> He worked here **from** 1997 **to** 2002.
> She'll be in Europe **from** June **until** August.

exercise 15-1

Select the preposition that best completes each sentence.

1. They left the theater **on/before/until** the end of the film.

2. I should be home **during/for/by** ten o'clock.

3. She only works **from/at/for** nine to three.

4. We always have a picnic **on/in/to** the Fourth of July.

5. Do you always eat lunch **for/since/at** noon?

6. Bill has been sad **for/since/at** his fortieth birthday.

7. Aunt Jane came to town **in/on/for** Carmen's big party.

8. We do a lot of shopping **during/on/by** the holiday season.

9. It's coldest here from December **to/at/on** February.

10. I'm afraid that we'll have to wait **to/until/since** tomorrow.

exercise   15-2

Fill in the blank with any appropriate word or phrase that expresses time.

1. The children were very noisy during _____.

2. We can expect Jim here for _____.

3. It's very rainy from May to _____.

4. I haven't seen you since _____.

5. Can you stay with me until _____?

6. Tom works hard _____ morning to night.

7. They wanted to leave work before _____.

8. The doctor gave him a checkup after _____.

9. Try to get here by _____.

10. His family usually stays at the lake in _____.

11. The twins were born on _____.

12. Dark shadows covered the ground at _____.

13. They were living in Europe during _____.

14. He's had a job in the city since _____.

15. They want to start the marathon by _____.

exercise   15-3

Write original sentences with the prepositional phrases given in parentheses.

1. (from noon until midnight) _____

2. (by June) _____

3. (since the end of winter) _____

4. (in spring) _____

5. (on May tenth) _____

6. (after 11:00 P.M.) _____

7. (before next year) _____

8. (during his lifetime) _____

9. (after dark) _____

10. (at sunset) _____

Compound Prepositions

When two or more words are strung together and end with *to, of,* or sometimes *from,* they are called *compound prepositions.* They function like all other prepositions. The only difference is that they are composed of more than a single word. Here is a list of the compound prepositions:

according to	in reference to
ahead of	in regard to
apart from	in spite of
because of	instead of
by means of	on account of
by way of	out of
in back of	up to
in front of	with respect to

Look at their use in a sentence and at the meaning that is derived:

Use in a Sentence	Meaning
According to Jim, the plan is perfect.	Jim's opinion
The project was completed **ahead of** schedule.	before expected, earlier than scheduled
Apart from a few complaints, everyone was satisfied.	except for a few complaints
Work stopped **because of** the storm.	the cause was the storm
The problem was solved **by means of** a complex formula.	by using a complex formula
Take a look at these examples **by way of** a contrast.	as a contrast
A stranger stood **in front of** me.	before me
No one was **in back of** us.	behind us

I gave this response **in regard to** his letter.
We pointed out the law that is **in reference to** this crime.
In spite of the blizzard, we drove all the way home.
Instead of a long dress, she chose a short one.
He stayed in bed **on account of** his cold.
The girl suddenly ran **out of** the room.
The little boy stepped **up to** the microphone.
With respect to all these losses, I have a few
harsh words to say.

concerning his letter
concerning this crime
not caring about the blizzard
not choosing a long dress
the cause was his cold
from inside the room
approached the microphone
concerning all these losses

exercise 16-1

Select the preposition that best completes each sentence.

1. Some men stood **in front of/instead of/up to** the store.

2. **Out of/By means of/According to** the forecast, it's going to rain today.

3. **By way of/Ahead of/In reference to** his remark, I just said, "Shame."

4. We stayed home **because of/out of/in regard to** the power outage.

5. Do you still live **with respect to/in back of/by way of** the shop?

6. There **ahead of/because of/on account of** us stood a large bison.

7. He quickly drove **by means of/out of/apart from** the driveway.

8. I was too nervous to walk **up to/in regard to/by way of** the president.

9. It happened **instead of/by means of/on account of** your carelessness!

10. She can't comment **in regard to/according to/up to** that matter.

exercise 16-2

Fill in the blank with any appropriate word or phrase.

1. Please write a report in reference to _____.

2. In spite of _____, she continued to love him.

3. In regard to _____, I have a statement to make.

4. I bought a compact car instead of _____.

5. Who's waiting in front of _____?

6. The man was arrested on account of _____.

7. There were several tables and chairs in back of _____.

8. A strange smell came out of _____.

9. I sent her some flowers by way of _____.

10. A baby rabbit hopped up to _____.

11. You can get to the top of the mountain by means of _____.

12. With respect to _____, some changes have to be made.

13. Apart from _____, everyone else will be fired.

14. According to _____, we're in a heat wave.

15. I could see a winding road ahead of _____.

exercise   16-3

Write original sentences with the prepositional phrases given in parentheses.

1. (ahead of time) _____

2. (because of an illness) _____

3. (in front of the factory) _____

4. (in reference to your last report) _____

5. (instead of a check) _____

6. (out of the clouds) _____

7. (with respect to his last wishes) _____

8. (according to the almanac) _____

9. (apart from a few friends) _____

10. (by means of the subway) _____

11. (in back of the garage) _____

12. (in spite of the darkness) _____

13. (on account of his riches) _____

14. (up to the river) _____

15. (in regard to these lies) _____

Prepositions That Combine with Other Words

Adverbs modify verbs and answer the questions *where, when,* and *how* of the action of the verb:

The sick girl remained **upstairs**. → Where did the sick girl remain?

The books arrived **today**. → When did the books arrive?

Bill ran **slowly**. → How did Bill run?

Often prepositions combine with another word to form a commonly used adverb. Prepositions in this form are frequently used as prefixes. Look at these examples:

Adverb	**Meaning**
by and by	soon
by and large	mostly, generally
downstairs	one floor below
indoors	in a building
inside	in the interior
outdoors	in the open air
outside	in the out-of-doors
underwater	beneath the surface of the water
up-country	toward the interior of the land
uphill	going up an incline
upstairs	one floor above
uptown	toward the center of the town

Sometimes the combination of a preposition and another word forms a noun:

Noun	Meaning
bylaw	an organization's rule
bypass	a detour
downfall	collapse, ruin
infield	the inner playing area in baseball
insight	understanding
outbreak	sudden or violent appearance
outgrowth	something that grows out of something else
outline	a preliminary or general plan
outlook	view, foresight
underarm	the area under the arm beneath the shoulder
underclassman	a freshman or sophomore in a school
underwear	garments worn under the clothes
upheaval	something rising up suddenly or violently
uproar	violent noise, tumult

At other times the combination of a preposition and another word results in a verb:

Verb	Meaning
install	establish or place in position
intone	recite in a monotone, give inflection
outdo	exceed, surpass
outline	draw the border, sketch
outlive	live longer than someone else
undergo	bear up under stress and survive
upgrade	raise to a higher level
uphold	raise, support, encourage
upset	overturn or disquiet someone

Adjectives are also formed in this way:

Adjective	Meaning
bygone	from a past time
down-and-out	poor or hopeless
downcast	looking downward or in low spirits
downhearted	discouraged, dejected
ingrown	having grown into the flesh
inland	land away from the sea
together	with each other, jointly
underage	not of legal age
undercover	secret, engaged in spying
upstanding	respectable, honest
up-to-date	modern, fashionable

The four preceding lists are only a small sampling of the many words that are derived from a preposition combining with another word. When you encounter such words, it is sometimes possible to analyze the meaning of the preposition and the meaning of the word with which it has been combined in order to determine the meaning of the new word. Consider these examples:

(**up** = rising upward + **grade** = level) = **to upgrade** (to raise to a higher level)
(**down** = going downward + **fall** = stumble) = **downfall** (collapse, ruin)

Keeping this in mind, you can sometimes guess the meaning of new words that are formed when a preposition is used as a prefix.

exercise 17-1

Select the word that best completes each sentence.

1. The strange woman was an **undercover/downstairs/upheaval** agent.

2. The newly elected governor is a(n) **bygone/ingrown/upstanding** person.

3. She **underwent/upset/intoned** her voice with the anger she felt.

4. They decided to go **by and large/uptown/uphill** for dinner.

5. Did you follow our club's **insight/bylaws/outlook**?

6. Her views just aren't **up-to-date/underage/down-and-out**.

7. The hikers followed the creek **downstairs/up-country/by and by**.

8. The old man didn't want to **outline/outlive/outlook** his wife.

9. My aunt **underwent/installed/upheld** a serious operation last year.

10. His look was **upstanding/bygone/downcast** and his face quite sad.

exercise 17-2

Fill in the blank with any appropriate word or phrase.

1. The new members refused to follow the bylaws _____.

2. Out in the street there was an uproar over _____.

3. While swimming underwater, he saw _____.

4. They were flying coach class but wanted to upgrade _____.

5. An underage girl came into _____.

6. The brothers were always trying to outdo _____.

7. The road uphill was _____.

8. There was a sudden outbreak of _____.

9. You need a technician to install _____.

10. The downhearted young man began to _____.

11. The couple lives downstairs from _____.

12. The underclassmen in _____ behaved badly.

13. I didn't mean to upset _____.

14. The undercover agent hid _____.

15. Within hours there was a total downfall of _____.

exercise 17-3

Write original sentences with the words or phrases given in parentheses.

1. (outdoors) _____

2. (to a bypass) _____

3. (intone) _____

4. (ingrown toenail) _____

5. (by and large) _____

6. (insight) _____

7. (his underarms) _____

8. (underwear) _____

9. (outline) _____

10. (uphold the law) _____

11. (inland) _____

12. (uptown) _____

13. (upheaval) _____

14. (undergo) _____

15. (upstanding person) _____

Participial Prepositions

This is a small category of prepositions but one that has some important uses. The present participial form of certain verbs, *although not true prepositions*, sometimes *have the characteristic of a preposition* and are used as one. Present participles are formed by adding *-ing* to the verb: *go* → *going, sing* → *singing, buy* → *buying*, etc.

Only certain present participles can act as prepositions:

concerning	following
considering	regarding
excluding	

Their use as a preposition is different from their use as a verb form. Take careful note of the differences:

This is **concerning** to me. = participle used as an adjective

He often wrote me **concerning** this problem. = preposition (about this problem)

The club was **considering** buying new equipment. = present participle

The group spent hours **considering** this issue. = preposition (on this issue)

Why are you **excluding** our old friends? = present participle

We shall meet every Tuesday **excluding** the first Tuesday in May. = preposition (except the first Tuesday in May)

An old woman was **following** us. = present participle

The show will go on **following** one more rehearsal. = preposition (after one more rehearsal)

Do you have details **regarding** this case? = participle used as an adjective

She finally spoke up **regarding** her son's behavior. = preposition (about her son's behavior)

exercise   18-1

Rewrite each sentence changing the italicized preposition to a participial preposition.

1. We'll need to put in a lot of time *on* this problem.

   _____

2. I had a lot to tell *about* the crimes he had committed.

   _____

3. I wanted to speak to her *about* our future together.

   _____

4. Maria passed every test *except* the one in math.

   _____

5. The picnic will go on as planned *after* the rainstorm.

   _____

exercise   18-2

Write two original sentences with the words in parentheses. One should contain a present participle; the other should contain a present participle used as a preposition.

1. (concerning)

   _____

   _____

2. (considering)

   _____

   _____

3. (excluding)

   _____

   _____

4. (following)

   _____

   _____

Postpositive Prepositions

This is another very small category of prepositions. They are derived from the shortened form of the preposition *toward*, which is *-ward*. *Postpositive* means that the prepositional form *-ward* occurs as a suffix. Notice how often another preposition acts as the prefix (*up, down, in, out*). Look at these examples:

backward	landward
downward	leeward
forward	outward
heavenward	seaward
homeward	upward
inward	windward

The points on a compass can also be combined with this suffix: *westward, eastward, northward, southward, southeastward.*

In each case, the word is adjectival or adverbial and means *in the direction of.* For example:

heavenward = in the direction of heaven

homeward = in the direction of home

seaward = in the direction of the sea

Two words that may be unfamiliar to you are *leeward* and *windward*. They do not conform precisely to the general meaning of this category of words. *Leeward* means *the direction in which the wind is blowing.* *Windward* means *the direction from which the wind is coming.*

Here are some sample sentences with each of these new words:

He walked **backward** without tripping.

When he looked **downward**, he saw a valley.

Tom moved **forward** a little in the crowded bus.

The balloons slowly rose **heavenward**.

Tomorrow I'm **homeward** bound!
You have to look **inward** to understand yourself.
The little boat drifted **landward**.
We sailed **leeward** into the sunset.
His **outward** appearance is good, but he's a nasty man.
Our ship moved **seaward** out of the little harbor.
When I looked **upward**, I saw the streaks of pink in the sky.
A steamer can travel **windward** with ease.
The troops marched **westward** toward the front lines.

exercise   19-1

Write two original sentences with the words in parentheses.

1. (backward)

   _____

   _____

2. (downward)

   _____

   _____

3. (homeward)

   _____

   _____

4. (inward)

   _____

   _____

5. (upward)

   _____

   _____

6. (windward)

   _____

   _____

7. (eastward)

   _____

   _____

Words That Require a Specific Preposition

Prepositions have a precise use. They cannot be used randomly but rather serve a particular function. As already discussed, some show a location. Others indicate a movement or a direction. In fact, there are some words and phrases that require a specific preposition in order to achieve the proper meaning. For example, you have to use the preposition *in* with the words *interested* or *interest*. Other prepositions make no sense:

CORRECT: I'm very interested **in** computer technology.

INCORRECT: Have you always been interested **about** classical music?

CORRECT: She shows no interest **in** such things.

INCORRECT: Tom has a great deal of interest **of** sports.

The same is true with many other words, most of which appear in verb phrases. Here is a list of commonly used expressions that require a specific preposition:

to ask for	to long for
to be alarmed by	to look after
to be capable of	to look at
to be generous with	to look for
to be interested in/interest in	to look forward to
to be sure of	to plead for/plea for
to beg for	to rely (up)on
to belong to	to speak about/of
to care about	to think about/of
to care for	to wait for

to depend (up)on

to dream about/of

to forget about

to hope for

to listen to

to walk up to

to watch over

to wish for

to worry about

most passive structures + by

Several phrases use the preposition *for* to complete their meaning. Whatever follows the preposition becomes the object of the preposition and forms a prepositional phrase. Look at the examples that follow:

Juan *asked* **for** a second helping of potatoes. (ask for = request)
The dog *begged* **for** a treat.
Maria *is caring* **for** her sick mother. (care for = tend to)
Jim really *cares* **for** Barbara. (care for = feel affection)
The crowd *was hoping* **for** a win, but the team lost.
Their family *longed* **for** a vacation in Europe.
They spent hours *looking* **for** the lost kitten.
She *pleaded* with the judge **for** mercy.
The lawyer made a brilliant *plea* **for** justice in this case.
How long do we have *to wait* **for** a bus?
The little boy *wished* **for** a new bicycle.

There are many phrases that begin with *to be.* They usually include an adjective or a participle, and each one requires the use of a specific preposition:

The woman *was* suddenly *alarmed* **by** the threat of a storm.
I didn't think you *were capable* **of** such a terrible thing.
Mr. Garcia *is* always so *generous* **with** his time.
She's not *interested* **in** old movies.
I'm developing an *interest* **in** science.
How can you *be sure* **of** what to do next?

Phrases that require *to*:

That red car *belongs* **to** me. (belongs to = ownership)
Tom wants *to belong* **to** our sports club. (belong to = membership)
I *listened* **to** the speaker's remarks with great interest.
Everyone *is looking forward* **to** the start of vacation.
A beautiful woman *walked up* **to** me and shook my hand.

Phrases that require *about*:

My brother *cares* a lot **about** his girlfriend.
Last night I *dreamt* **about** our trip to Alaska.
She says she'll never *forget* **about** me.
You shouldn't *speak* **about** such things!
It seems I'm always *thinking* **about** food.
My parents still *worry* **about** my sister and me.

Phrases that require *on* or *upon*:

You can always *depend* **(up)on** us.
There's no one here that I can *rely* **(up)on**.

Phrases that require *of.* Notice that these phrases are often the same ones that use *about:*

> The dog seemed to be *dreaming* **of** chasing a rabbit.
> Someone *was speaking* **of** the new boss's bad temper.
> Guess what I'm *thinking* **of.**

The verb *to look* forms two new expressions with the prepositions *after* (meaning "to care for") and *at:*

> The men stayed home *to look* **after** the children.
> They *were looking* upward **at** the stars in the sky.

When the verb *watch* is combined with the preposition *over,* it means "to tend to" and "to protect":

> The shepherd *watched* **over** the nervous flock of sheep.

When an active sentence is changed to a passive sentence, the subject of the active sentence becomes the object of the preposition *by* in the passive sentence:

> Active: A thief stole the wallet.
> Passive: The wallet was stolen **by** the thief.

Here are a few more examples of sentences in the passive voice:

> Active: A raging fire destroyed the house.
> Passive: The house *was destroyed* **by** a raging fire.

> Active: The proud father tucks the little girl into bed.
> Passive: The little girl *is tucked* into bed **by** the proud father.

> Active: The chief of police himself had warned them.
> Passive: They *had been warned* **by** the chief of police himself.

> Active: Will a new chef prepare dinner?
> Passive: Will dinner *be prepared* **by** a new chef?

exercise 20-1

Select the word that best completes each sentence.

1. I began to beg my father **of/about/for** more money.

2. She was being followed **by/to/for** a strange man.

3. Juanita also **depends/belongs/wishes** to our club now.

4. Don't you want to **watch/ask/care** for a little help?

5. I never stop worrying **for/of/about** my daughter.

6. I really care **by/at/for** her. I'm in love.

7. Tom has absolutely no interest **at/in/to** jazz.

8. It's difficult for them to forget **of/(up)on/about** the war.

9. I know I can **rely/hope/plead** on your honesty.

10. I **long/walk/dream** for a good night's sleep.

11. She was deeply hurt **to/over/by** his insults.

12. The child is hardly capable **of/for/(up)on** hurting anyone.

13. I'll **worry/wait/plead** for you in front of the theater.

14. You shouldn't be so generous **with/for/at** us.

15. Are you looking forward **for/at/to** the party?

exercise   20-2

Fill in the blank with any appropriate word or phrase.

1. He became alarmed by _____.

2. You shouldn't worry about _____.

3. These women are very interested in _____.

4. I'm going to wish for _____.

5. Are you absolutely sure of _____?

6. The immigration officer walked up to _____.

7. Does this jacket belong to _____?

8. You're always thinking about _____.

9. How can I depend on _____?

10. The wounded soldier was pleading for _____.

11. Never forget about _____.

12. The barn was blown down by _____.

13. We need a guard to watch over _____.

14. You should listen to _____.

15. A large animal was looking at _____.

exercise   20-3

Fill in the blank with the appropriate phrase. Choose from the phrases in this unit that require a specific preposition. Write all your sentences in the past tense.

EXAMPLE: My uncle *was interested in* American history.

1. The young man _____ me with a gift in his hand.

2. The orator _____ the importance of saving money.

3. I think this umbrella _____ to Aunt Norma.

4. I _____ the exam! I'm going to fail for sure!

5. If you needed anything, you always _____ me.

6. A police officer _____ the injured pedestrian.

7. Where were you? I _____ you for two hours!

8. Dad _____ me, but I knew how to take care of myself.

9. The boys _____ the missing child for several hours.

10. Jim _____ an extra ten dollars but got nothing.

exercise   20-4

Write original sentences with the phrases given in parentheses.

1. (to be capable of) _____

2. (to look for) _____

3. (a passive structure + by) _____

4. (no interest in) _____

5. (to wish for) _____

6. (a plea for) _____

7. (to be sure of) _____

8. (to rely upon) _____

9. (to beg for) _____

10. (to look forward to) _____

11. (to care about) _____

12. (to hope for) _____

13. (to look after) _____

14. (to dream of) _____

15. (a passive structure + by) _____

Prepositions and Phrasal Verbs

This is a very large category of verbal expressions that use prepositions to change the meaning of a verb. It is different from the ordinary combination of a verb and a preposition because the verb-plus-preposition phrase as a whole acquires a completely new meaning and one that is often radically different from the original meaning of the verb.

Here are a few sentences with the verb *to come* used with its regular meaning. Each one has a prepositional phrase in it, but the meaning of *to come* is not changed:

These young people **come from** Spain.

He **came into** the room and sat down.

Come with me, please.

Now look at these sentences with *to come* and a preposition. The meaning of the verb *to come* is changed:

The man **came to** after a few minutes. (He regained consciousness.)

Tom finally **came around** and signed the contract. (He changed his mind.)

How did you **come up with** this idea? (How did you create this idea?)

Verbs that change their meaning when combined with one or more prepositions are called *phrasal verbs*. They are numerous in English and are an important element of grammar. It is essential to identify them and to be able to understand the new meanings that are derived by their formation. Let's look at some important phrasal verbs.

VERB + PREPOSITIONS

Ask

The regular verb *to ask* means "to pose a question" or "to make a request." That meaning is altered when the verb is combined with certain prepositions. In phrasal verbs those prepositions are sometimes called *particles*. You will notice that the particle-prepositions are often used as adverbs.

The phrasal verb *to ask around* means "to seek information from a variety of sources." The particle *about* is sometimes used in place of *around*:

> I **asked around** about the new girl and learned she was from Poland.
> **Ask around** and you'll learn where you can rent a cheap apartment.
> **Ask about** and you'll discover where there's a nice place to eat.

The phrasal verb *to ask out* has changed its meaning again. It now means "to invite someone to go somewhere" or "to invite on a date." It suggests that someone is romantically interested in another person:

> John **asked** Maria **out**, but she refused.
> I was too shy **to ask** her **out**.
> The handsome man was **asked out** by his friend's cousin.

Be

You are already familiar with the verb *to be*. It shows the existence of someone or something (*They are here.*) or helps to describe a condition or quality (*I am old.*). It is an irregular verb and is the only English verb that has a complex conjugation in the present and past tenses:

Present		Past	
I am	we are	I was	we were
you are	you are	you were	you were
he, she, it is	they are	he, she, it was	they were

Its participle is *been: I have been, you have been, he has been,* and so on.

The verb *to be* is also used as an auxiliary with a present participle to show a continuing action:

> I am singing.
> You were writing.
> They have been studying.
> Tom will be working.

But the meaning of the verb is altered when it is used in certain phrases. Let's look at some examples of phrasal verbs formed from this verb.

The verb *to be in* has a very specific meaning. It says that someone is at home or available at the office:

> **I'm in** for the night.
> **Is** Dr. Jones **in** this afternoon?
> Tell my client that I won't **be in** until eight in the morning.

The opposite of *to be in* is *to be out*. It says that someone is not at home or not available at the office:

> John **is out** and won't be home until late.
> I believe Dr. Jones **is out** for the day. He'll be in the office at 8:00 A.M. tomorrow.

In the phrasal verb *to be on,* only the preposition *on* has been added, but the meaning is completely changed by it. This verb means that some apparatus, machinery, or equipment is functioning. It is the opposite of *to be off*:

> Press the green button, and the machine **is on**. Press the red button, and the machine **is off**.
> It's hot in here. **Is** the air conditioning **on**?
> The engine is so quiet that I can't tell if it **is on**.

Use *to be out of sight* to say that you can no longer see someone or something or that someone or something is no longer in your range of vision:

> He ran up the hill and **was** soon **out of sight**.
> In a couple more minutes the ship **will be out of sight**.
> The rocket **was out of sight** in just a matter of seconds.

The verb *to be with it* has two specific meanings. One describes a person who is very contemporary and in fashion. The other suggests that a person is in a good state of mind and is thinking properly:

> Mary has another new dress. She **is** always so **with it**.
> Your hairdo is old fashioned. Why can't you **be** more **with it**?
> John drank a lot last night and **isn't with it** today.
> I forget everything. **I'm** just not **with it** anymore.

Use *to be onto something* to say that someone is discovering something important or has an important idea. It also suggests that someone has found a clue that will help to solve a problem:

> What a great invention! **You're** really **onto something**!
> I read her article about stopping pollution. I think **she's onto something**.
> Look at the map I found. **We're** finally **onto something** that will help to find the treasure.

The verb *to be up to something* says that someone looks suspicious and has some kind of evil intentions. It is sometimes stated as *to be up to no good*:

> What's that man doing? I think **he's up to something**.
> I knew you **were up to something** when I saw you holding a shovel.
> Her children **are** always **up to no good**.

exercise 21-1

Select the word or phrase that best completes each sentence.

1. It's cold. The heat **ask**/**on**/**is** probably off.

2. If you ask **around**/**with**/**out**, you'll get his address.

3. The old woman was **up to/onto/about** something again.

4. She was too timid to **be/ask/out of** Juan out.

5. The scientist knew she was **onto/out of/up** something.

6. My lawyer won't be **off/out of sight/in** until noon.

7. Your parents are so up-to-date and **onto something/with it/around**.

8. Why was the TV **on/out/up to something** all night?

9. The detective believed she was up **with it/to no good/and around**.

10. He wants to take a shower but the water is **on/onto/off** again.

---

exercise   21-2

Fill in the blank with any appropriate word or phrase taken from the phrasal verbs formed from ask *and* be.

1. I wanted to know who he was and _____ about him.

2. The jumbo jet was quickly _____.

3. The burglar was obviously _____ no good.

4. What time will Professor Gomez _____ in?

5. Did your nephew _____ my niece out?

6. Having found a clue, they knew they were _____.

7. If the fan _____, why is it so hot in here?

8. When he turned to look, her train was already out _____.

9. Use makeup! Color your hair! Try to be _____!

10. The dentist is _____ for the day.

Come

You're already familiar with this verb of motion that means "to approach, to move toward, or to arrive." Its conjugation is irregular and has these principal parts:

	Present	Past	Present Perfect	Future
you	come	came	have come	will come
he, she, it	comes	came	has come	will come

Four distinct meanings are derived from the phrasal verb *to come through (for) (with)*: (1) to endure or survive, (2) to be approved by some official body or institution, (3) to perform a helpful service for someone, and (4) to produce something that has been promised. Check these examples:

> Somehow they **came through** the storm without a scratch.
> Your loan **came through** and you'll receive a check in the mail.
> Mom always **came through for** me whenever I had a problem.
> Tom will never **come through with** the money he promised.

With the particle *to*, *come to* has a simple new meaning: to become conscious again or to wake up:

> Her eyes opened and she slowly **came to**.
> The old man fell asleep and never **came to** again.

The verb *to come up with* means "to find someone or something that someone needs." Look at these examples:

> I'll try **to come up with** a piano player for your party.
> She **came up with** another good idea.

The phrasal verb *to come upon* means "to happen upon someone or something." The particle *on* is sometimes used in place of *upon*:

> When she **comes on** her brother, she'll have the shock of her life.
> I **came upon** an interesting book in the library.

Get

This complicated verb has two basic meanings: "to receive" and "to become." But it is used in many other phrases and its meaning is altered each time. It's irregular and has these principal parts:

	Present	Past	Present Perfect	Future
you	get	got	have gotten	will get
he, she, it	gets	got	has gotten	will get

In this form, *to get back (at)* has two new meanings: (1) to return from someplace, and (2) using the preposition *at*, to seek revenge upon a person or group. Look at these examples:

> When did you **get back** from Mexico? Become.
> He said he'd **get back at** you for lying about him.
> The terrorist wanted **to get back at** the government.

To *get behind (in)* has two meanings: (1) to promote or support someone or some activity, and (2) using the preposition *in*, to be late or lagging behind in performing a task. Here are some examples:

> You have **to get behind** your candidate, if you want him to win the election.
> I'm **getting behind in** my work again.
> If you **get behind in** your exercising, you'll put on weight again.

To get in on means "to participate in an event or to receive a share in something because of that participation." Some examples:

> You'll need an invitation, if you want **to get in on** the conference.
> I **got in on** the deal to sell farming equipment in Canada.

The phrase *to get into it* doesn't reveal what it means by the makeup of the words. Its new meaning is "to have an argument or a fight." Look at these examples:

> John **got into it** with another driver over a parking space.
> My parents always **get into it** over money.

In this form the phrasal verb *to get off* has two meanings: (1) often using the preposition *of*, to depart from your job, and (2) to have a person cleared of criminal wrongdoing. Some examples:

> I **got off** early and came straight home.
> What time will you **get off of** work tomorrow?
> The clever lawyer **got** the burglar **off** with a small fine.
> I'm innocent! You have **to get** me **off**!

Phrasal Verbs as Participles

The phrasal verbs *to get back, to get into,* and *to get off* can act as the participle in a passive voice sentence:

> Her jewelry was never **gotten back**.

> The room was **gotten into** by a clever thief.

> The crook was **gotten off** by a shrewd lawyer.

With the particle *on, to get on (with)* has three meanings: (1) to cooperate and thrive with somebody, (2) often with the phrase *in years* it means to grow old, and (3) using the preposition *with*, to continue with something. Some examples:

> The two former enemies seemed **to be getting on** without a problem.
> My grandparents **are getting on in years**.
> The crisis is over. Now we have **to get on with** our lives.

 **exercise**   **21-3**

Select the word or phrase that best completes each sentence.

1. Jim came through **with/for/up** me again.

2. Let's get on **to/with/back to** the meeting.

3. The drowsy woman came **to/onto/up with** very slowly.

4. The children came **upon/off/at** a little cottage in the woods.

5. I work all afternoon. I get **back at/into it/off at** 5:00 P.M.

6. Ms. Brown **came up/comes to/has come upon** with a wonderful slogan.

7. Hurry! You're **getting/got/coming** behind in your work.

8. How can I get **behind in/on with/in on** this deal?

9. The two boys got **back at/into it/up with** after school.

10. She got **back at/up with/on with** us for gossiping.

exercise   21-4

Fill in the blank with any appropriate word or phrase taken from the phrasal verbs formed from come *and* get.

1. Start the music. Let's get _____ the show.

2. I don't want to stay in jail! Please _____ me off!

3. Mr. Brown finally _____ with our loan.

4. They were arguing over the accident and soon _____ it.

5. Maybe she'll come _____ if you give her some water.

6. Jim _____ an old magazine in the attic.

7. Did Maria get _____ the stock purchase?

8. We all _____ Ms. Brown, and she won the election.

9. The car dealer eventually came through _____ us.

10. I _____ at six. You can pick me up then.

Keep

This is an irregular verb that means "to retain, maintain, or cause to continue." Look at its principal parts:

	Present	**Past**	**Present Perfect**	**Future**
you	keep	kept	have kept	will keep
he, she, it	keeps	kept	has kept	will keep

Followed by a present participle, *to keep on (with)* means "to continue doing something." Using the preposition *with* followed by a noun or pronoun, it also means "to continue doing something." Look at these examples:

> The professor told the students **to keep on** studying.
> The professor told the students **to keep on with** their studies.

To keep out (of) has three meanings: (1) to stay outside a place, (2) to remain neutral about something as in "minding one's own business," and (3) to stop someone from entering a place:

> **Keep out!** This means you!
> I want you **to keep out of** my office when I'm working.
> **Keep out of** this! This is none of your business!
> I want you **to keep** Ms. Johnson **out of** our meeting.

Three new meanings are derived by using *to keep to (oneself)*: (1) to maintain an agreed-upon plan or promise, and (2) to remain withdrawn and alone. If you add *something* to the phrase (*to keep something to oneself*), it has a third meaning: "to maintain a secret." Some examples:

> If we **keep to** our original plan, we'll achieve our goals.
> The old woman **kept** more and more **to herself.**
> Please **keep** this information **to yourself**. Don't tell anyone.

The phrasal verb *to keep up (with)* also has three meanings: (1) to hold someone or something upright, (2) to prevent a person from falling asleep, and (3) using the preposition *with*, to remain equal with someone or something. Look at these examples:

> **Keep** him **up**. Don't let him fall.
> He's very sleepy, but somehow we have **to keep** Jim **up** until midnight.
> I can't **keep up with** you. Walk slower.

Kick

Kick is a regular verb and means "to strike with a foot." Look what happens to its meaning when it becomes a phrasal verb.

The phrasal verb *to kick off* means "to start something" and comes from the start of a football game, which is the *kickoff*. It has a colloquial meaning that is casual and somewhat crude: "to pass away or die." This second meaning is used without compassion:

> Let's **kick off** the meeting with a few words from Ms. Johnson.
> The poor old man **kicked off** during the night.

In this form the verb *to kick out (of)* means "to evict someone or eject something from a place":

> Maria **kicked out** her boyfriend last night.
> I **kicked** the boxes **out of** my way.

Knock

This verb is regular. It means "to strike, hit, or rap."

With the particle *down*, *to knock down* means "to hit someone or something to the ground." Here are some examples:

> The bully **knocked** me **down** and ran off laughing.
> The wind is going **to knock down** that old fence.

In this form the verb *to knock off (it, work)* derives a few new meanings: (1) to stop doing something, (2) using the pronoun *it* to make a rather rude meaning, "to cease a certain behavior," (3) as a slang expression, "to murder a person," and (4) using the noun *work*, "to conclude the day's work." As a noun—*knockoff*—the word means "an imitation." Some examples:

> You can **knock off** digging. The plans have been changed.
> **Knock it off!** Acting like that isn't funny!
> The gangsters **knocked off** an old enemy.
> My father usually **knocks off work** around 6:00 P.M.
> He wanted a Rolex but bought a **knockoff** from a street vendor.

Look at the meanings that are derived for the verb *to knock out*: (1) to cause someone to become unconscious, (2) to develop or make something quickly, and (3) to cause something to stop functioning.

> Bill hit the man so hard that he **knocked** him **out**.
> That drink almost **knocked** me **out**.
> The workers **knocked out** a prototype in a matter of hours.
> A lightning strike **knocked out** the radio station.

Phrasal Verbs That Act as Nouns

The phrasal verbs *to kick off*, *to knock off*, and *to knock out* have a noun formation:

> This party is the **kickoff** to a week of celebrating.

> This isn't a Cartier. It's a **knockoff**.

> The champ won the boxing match by a **knockout**.

exercise	21-5

Select the word or phrase that best completes each sentence.

1. You run too fast. I can't keep **up with/to/out of** you.

2. With one blow, he knocked the man **on/out/it off.**

3. We have to **keep on/kick off/keep to** working until we're done.

4. The landlord kicked us **up with/off/out of** our apartment.

5. Knock **it/out/yourself** off. You're bothering me.

6. The carpenters **knocked down/kicked out of/kept up with** the wall in just a few minutes.

7. They kicked **out/out of/off** the parade with a patriotic march.

8. He was shot in the morning. He kicked **off/to/up with** in the afternoon.

9. What time do you knock **out/off/up with** work?

10. She's so lonely, yet she still keeps **up with us/off it/to herself**.

exercise	21-6

Fill in the blank with any appropriate word or phrase taken from the phrasal verbs formed from keep, kick, *and* knock.

1. The coach wanted them to _____ practicing.

2. Careful or you'll knock _____ the window!

3. How can we keep those kids _____ our yard?

4. You had better knock _____ before I get really angry.

5. If you keep _____ this road, you'll get there in an hour.

6. They had an argument, and she _____ him out.

7. The champ knocked his opponent _____, but he got up immediately.

8. If you pedal faster, you'll _____ with the other cyclists.

9. We'll _____ off the party with a few drinks.

10. What time do you _____ of work?

Put

To put is an irregular verb and means "to place or set." Its principal parts look like this:

	Present	**Past**	**Present Perfect**	**Future**
you	put	put	have put	will put
he, she, it	puts	put	has put	will put

The phrasal verb *to put down (for)* has four new meanings: (1) to cease holding someone or something up, (2) to ridicule or demean someone or something, (3) to write down, and (4) using the preposition *for*, to sign someone up to participate in something. Look at these examples:

> I don't want you to carry me. **Put** me **down**!
> I try very hard, but still you **put** me **down**. I can't do any better.
> The stenographer **put down** every word the lawyer said.
> Tim likes soccer. You can **put** him **down for** that.

In this form the verb *to put on* has three meanings: (1) to place on headgear or wear a certain garment, (2) to pretend, and (3) to tease someone. Some examples:

> The woman **put on** a new hat and dress and went to the party.
> He's not really sick. He's just **putting on**.
> It can't be true! You're **putting** me **on**! Anna is married again?

This phrasal verb *to put out (oneself, of)* also has various new meanings: (1) to generate an abundance of something (often used as a noun: *output*), (2) to annoy a person, (3) using a reflexive pronoun, to allow oneself to be inconvenienced or to do a favor for someone, and (4) to eject someone or something from a place.

> That new copy machine really **puts out**.
> What's the total **output** of this department each month?
> Professor Jones was really **put out** by all the silly questions.
> I really **put** myself **out** for you. Is this the thanks I get?
> Please **put** the dog **out**. I can't stand his barking.

To put up (with) has three new meanings: (1) to provide someone with housing (usually for one night), (2) to erect, and (3) using the preposition *with*, to tolerate someone or something:

> It's storming. We had better **put** you **up** for the night.
> We always **put up** the Christmas tree in early December.
> I can't **put up with** your lying and cheating anymore.

Quiet

Quiet is a regular verb that means "to make calm or silent." As a phrasal verb its meaning changes only slightly.

To quiet down means "to become calm or silent" or "to make someone calm or silent." Here are some examples:

> As the grieving woman came in, the room suddenly **quieted down**.
> Give the man a shot **to quiet** him **down**.

Rest

To rest is another regular verb. It means "to relax and enjoy an idle moment."

In the form *to rest up (from)*, the meaning of the verb is not altered greatly. With the particle *up*, the suggestion is that the goal is to rest completely and not just for a moment. With the preposition *from* you can tell what activity is avoided to provide rest:

> You're exhausted. I want you **to rest up** and leave everything else to me.
> I ache all over. I need **to rest up from** all this exercising.

exercise   21-7

Select the word or phrase that best completes each sentence.

1. Put me **on/up/down** for the refreshments committee.

2. The baby is feverish and won't **put/quiet/rest** down.

3. I need to rest up **for/with/from** all this exercise.

4. Carmen **rest up/put on/put up with** his lies for many years.

5. You're so hospitable, but don't **put down/put up/put yourself** out.

6. He's so excited, but he needs to quiet **on/up/down**.

7. I **rested up/quieted down/put up with** all morning and went to work at noon.

8. She's not sick! She's just putting **out/off/on**!

9. It can't be true! Are you **put/down for/putting** me on?

10. The janitor was **quieted down/put up with/put out by** all the garbage in the hallway.

exercise   21-8

Fill in the blank with any appropriate word or phrase taken from the phrasal verbs formed from put, quiet, *and* rest.

1. Why don't you _____? You've had a long day.

2. You're never satisfied with my work. You always _____ me down.

3. Spend the night here. We can put you _____.

4. When the class _____ down, I'll pass out the new material.

5. I love soccer. Put me _____ that team.

6. Tom _____ a dress and a wig for the Halloween party.

7. Anita can't put _____ his deceit any longer.

8. I think you should rest _____ that long trip.

9. He wished he could put his roommate _____ his house.

10. You can put the groceries _____ on that table.

Take

This is an irregular verb. It means "to receive, grasp, or accept." Look at its principal parts.

	Present	Past	Present Perfect	Future
you	take	took	have taken	will take
he, she, it	takes	took	has taken	will take

The combination of words *to take back (from)* has four meanings: (1) to return something, (2) to remind someone of something in the past, (3) to retract something that has been said or written, and (4) using the preposition *from*, to return something to the original owner from someone who had temporary possession of it. Some examples:

> I **took** the tools I borrowed **back** to Jim.
> Hearing that song **takes** me **back** to when I was still in college.
> **Take** that **back**! You're lying!
> She wants **to take back** the ring **from** me.

The phrasal verb *to take down (from)* has three new meanings: (1) to write something on paper, (2) to guide or transport someone or something to a place, (3) to dismantle or raze, and (4) using the preposition *from*, to remove someone or something from a high location. Look at these examples:

> **Take** the phone number **down** for me: 555-0884.
> Ms. Johnson **took** the reports **down** to the meeting.
> If you don't know the way, I can **take** you **down** there.
> They're going **to take down** the old movie palace.
> Anna **takes** a box of letters **down from** the shelf.

To take in has three meanings: (1) to decrease the size of a garment, (2) to give someone shelter, and (3) to fool someone. Here are some examples:

> I've lost some weight. I need **to take** these pants **in**.
> My parents **took** the homeless man **in** for the night.
> Robert **took** me **in** with one of his silly schemes again.

Another phrasal verb can be used with three different prepositions. *To take off (after, for, of)* has a variety of meanings: (1) to remove a garment, (2) often using the word *day*, to stay home from school or work, (3) to leave the ground in flight, (4) using the preposition *after*, to run in the direction of someone or something, (5) using the preposition *for*, to depart for a place, and (6) using the preposition *of*, to remove from a place.

The doctor asked me **to take off** my shirt.
I felt ill, so I **took the day off**.
The jet fighters **took off** in a matter of minutes.
When he saw the prowler, Mike **took off after** him.
Last night Jim and Maria **took off for** Vancouver.
She **took** a spider **off of** the piano.

To take on has three meanings: (1) to accept, (2) to hire, and (3) to become emotional about something.

You always **take on** too much work.
If you **take on** Bill, he'll work as hard as two men.
Anna often **takes on** about the death of her husband.

The verb *to take over (from)* has four new meanings: (1) to take control of a business, (2) to accept responsibility for something, (3) to deliver something, and (4) using the preposition *from*, to assume control of something from someone. Some examples:

The corporation **took over** two smaller companies.
Can you **take over** the Johnson account? They need someone like you.
I **took** the CD player **over** to Maria's house.
We're taking over the travel agency **from** Mr. Gomez.

Another phrasal verb with a variety of meanings is *to take up (with, on)*. It means (1) to raise the hem of a garment, (2) often using the preposition *with*, to discuss a person or issue, (3) to be involved in a special skill or hobby, (4) using the preposition *with*, to have an affair with someone, (5) using the preposition *on*, to agree to someone's proposal or offer. Look at these examples:

That dress is too long. **Take** it **up** a couple inches.
The committee **took up** the problem of recycling plastics.
I need **to take up** the question of Jim's employment **with** you.
My daughter **has taken up** stamp collecting.
My ex-wife **is taking up with** a man from Texas.
I'd like **to take** them **up on** their offer to buy my house.

Talk

Talk is a regular verb. It means "to speak or to converse."

With the particle *back*, *to talk back* means "to respond to someone rudely or disrespectfully." Some examples:

The boy has no fear of **talking back** to his father.
You shouldn't **talk back** to a teacher like that.

Phrasal Verbs That Act as Nouns

The verbs *to take down, to take off, to take over,* and *to talk back* have a noun formation. Nouns can often also act as adjectives.

> The wrestling match was over with two quick **takedowns**. (noun)
>
> **Takeoff** can be a dangerous time for an aircraft. (noun)
>
> The **takeoff** distance is 1,500 meters. (noun used as adjective)
>
> The **takeover** of our firm came as a surprise. (noun)
>
> We learned of the **takeover** bid too late. (noun used as adjective)
>
> **Talking back** to a parent is a terrible thing. (noun)

To talk someone into means "to convince someone of something":

> You'll never **talk** me **into** investing in that stock.
> Juan can **talk** anyone **into** anything.

The verb *to talk over* has two new meanings: (1) to discuss someone or something with another person, and (2) to use a microphone while speaking.

> We have **to talk over** Barbara's recent behavior.
> They're going **to talk** the matter **over** after lunch.
> My boss loves **talking over** a microphone.

Phrasal Verbs as Participles

The phrasal verbs *to take back, to take down, to take in, to take off, to take on, to take over, to take up,* and *to talk over* can act as the participle in a passive voice sentence:

> The books **are being taken back** by Tim.
>
> The drapes **have been taken down** for cleaning.
>
> They **were taken in** by his smooth talk.
>
> The vases **will be taken off** the shelf.
>
> The new girl **was taken on** last week.
>
> Why **was** this firm **taken over**?
>
> Your hemline should **be taken up** a bit.
>
> The matter **will be talked over** in a private meeting.

exercise   21-9

Select the word or phrase that best completes each sentence.

1. Ms. Brown will take over **from/off/on** Mr. Jones.

2. Let's sit down and talk this problem **into/over/back**.

3. I took everything **off of/down/back from** her apartment.

4. You shouldn't **talk back/take back/take over** to your mother!

5. You're not going to talk me **over/into/back** that again.

6. I'll take **down/off of/on** the curtains and wash them.

7. The shelter **takes over from/takes down/takes in** homeless people.

8. Take **on/over/off** your coat and relax.

9. That skirt is long. Let's take it **up/off/over from**.

10. My brother **takes over/took up/has taken in** with my ex-girlfriend.

exercise   21-10

Fill in the blank with any appropriate word or phrase taken from the phrasal verbs formed from take *and* talk.

1. A new company took _____ the factory.

2. His store is _____ several new employees.

3. _____ back to a teacher is terrible behavior.

4. In the summer the students took off _____ California.

5. Your waist is smaller. You should take _____ your pants.

6. I'd like to take you _____ your offer.

7. Anita _____ me into going to the dance with her.

8. The reporter took _____ every word I said.

9. You ought to _____ what you said to her.

10. No one talked it _____ with me.

Remember These Separable Phrasal Verbs

Sometimes *particles* have two possible positions in a sentence with a phrasal verb when the direct object in the sentence is a noun: after the object or before the object. But when the object is a pronoun, it has only one position: after the object.

You encountered these separable phrasal verbs: *to kick off, to kick out, to knock down, to knock off, to knock out, to put down, to put on, to put up, to quiet down, to take back, to take down, to take in, to take off, to take on, to take over, to take up,* and *to talk over.* In these verbs the particles are *back, down, in, off, on, out, over,* and *up.* Look at these examples that show the position of the particle with nouns and pronouns:

He kicked his shoes **off**.
He kicked **off** his shoes.
He kicked them **off**.

We knocked the wall **down**.
We knocked **down** the wall.
We knocked it **down**.

Jim knocked the bully **out**.
Jim knocked **out** the bully.
Jim knocked him **out**.

Put that dress **on**.
Put **on** that dress.
Put it **on**.

I can't quiet the boy **down**.
I can't quiet **down** the boy.
I can't quiet him **down**.

We took the curtains **down**.
We took **down** the curtains.
We took them **down**.

John takes his shoes **off**.
John takes **off** his shoes.
John takes them **off**.

Their company took our company **over**.
Their company took **over** our company.
Their company took us **over**.

Let's talk the problem **over**.
Let's talk **over** the problem.
Let's talk it **over**.

She kicked the woman **out**.
She kicked **out** the woman.
She kicked her **out**.

I knocked his hat **off**.
I knocked **off** his hat.
I knocked it **off**.

I put the baby **down**.
I put **down** the baby.
I put her **down**.

We put a shelf **up**.
We put **up** a shelf.
We put it **up**.

Take what you said **back**!
Take **back** what you said!
Take it **back**!

Mom takes the old woman **in**.
Mom takes **in** the old woman.
Mom takes her **in**.

Did they take another man **on**?
Did they take **on** another man?
Did they take him **on**?

Take the hem **up**.
Take **up** the hem.
Take it **up**.

exercise 21-11

Select the word or phrase that best completes each sentence.

1. Grandmother put on **it**/**an apron**.

2. We need to talk **it**/**these people** over.

3. I can't put up with **they/your insults**.

4. They'll kick off **them/the celebration** at ten o'clock.

5. We're going to take in **him/some boarders**.

6. The drug knocked **her/the doors** out.

7. Mr. Johnson took over **myself/our business**.

8. Put **we/the gun** down and turn around.

9. I'll measure the skirt and you take **it/the hem** in.

10. We need to quiet **he/your mother** down.

exercise   21-12

Write three original sentences with the phrasal verbs in parentheses. Use the same noun in the first two and place the particle in the two different positions that are possible. Use a pronoun in the third sentence. Follow the example.

EXAMPLE: (to put on)
He put his gloves on.
He put on his gloves.
He put them on.

1. (to knock down)

    _____

    _____

    _____

2. (to put up)

    _____

    _____

    _____

3. (to take over)

    _____

    _____

    _____

4. (to kick out)

_____

_____

_____

5. (to put down)

_____

_____

_____

6. (to take up)

_____

_____

_____

7. (to quiet down)

_____

_____

_____

8. (to knock off)

_____

_____

_____

You have had only a small sampling of phrasal verbs and the prepositions that help to form them. It is important to recognize phrasal verbs in order to determine their actual meaning. Frequently, someone who is learning English *assumes* the meaning of a sentence knowing the meaning of the basic verb in that sentence. But the verb could be a phrasal verb and, therefore, the meaning might escape the learner.

When you identify a phrasal verb in a sentence, look it up in a good dictionary. In the submeanings of the basic verb are often frequently used phrasal verbs. Here is a sample dictionary entry:

> **come** *verb* (**came, come, coming**) 1. to move to a place; to move here; to approach. 2. to arrive; to be present. **–to come about** 1. to happen or take place. 2. to turn to the opposite tack, as of a ship. **–to come to** 1. to revive; to regain consciousness. 2. to amount to

You will notice that *to come about* and *to come to* are both phrasal verbs, and the meaning of the phrases differ considerably from the meaning of the basic verb *come*. It is unwise to guess at the meaning of phrasal verbs. Rely on a good dictionary.

A Variety of Prepositional Uses

You have encountered a wide variety of prepositions and learned how they are used. The following exercises will give you practice in identifying these varieties and in using them in context.

exercise 22-1

Select the word or phrase that best completes each sentence.

1. We've been living in this house **because of/during/since/concerning** last March.

2. Coach is filled, but I can **to hope for/upgrade/agree with/into** you to first class.

3. The security guard **watched over/came up/agreed/agreed with** the new shipment of computers.

4. The electricity **gets on/on/came through with/has been off** for two days.

5. I often dream **about/for/on account of/off** my home in Ireland.

6. The frightened dog had been bitten **from/because/at/by** a snake.

7. The Constitution was finally ratified **by means of/by/at/on** this date.

8. I enjoy it here **along/at/in spite of/except** the bad weather.

9. There's a newspaper boy **of/at/on/onto** the front door.

10. We really look **at/forward to/with respect to/from** your next visit.

exercise 22-2

Complete each sentence with any appropriate phrase.

1. Why do you spend so much time with _____?

2. Several fans came rushing up to _____.

3. Who asked for _____?

4. I usually get off _____.

5. I learned not to depend upon _____.

6. They should be in Detroit on _____.

7. The ship docked at _____.

8. Maria can't seem to forget about _____.

9. The sleek sailboat headed seaward and _____.

10. The new golf clubs belong to _____.

11. My relatives will return to New York in _____.

12. I haven't been in Europe since _____.

13. Did you remain in the United States during _____?

14. According to _____, there's going to be a storm today.

15. Somehow the new employee came up with _____.

16. The embarrassed girl decided to get back at _____.

17. Our flight arrived ahead of _____.

18. I don't like waiting for _____.

19. _____ upset the poor woman.

20. _____ in the pasture.

21. _____ was soon out of sight.

22. _____ wanted to belong to our fraternity.

23. _____ out of the conference hall.

24. Apart from my own parents, _____.

25. _____ toward the covered bridge.

exercise   22-3

Write an original sentence for each word or phrase in parentheses.

1. (onto) _____

2. (because of) _____

3. (after) _____

4. (homeward) _____

5. (concerning) _____

6. (to be interested in) _____

7. (to keep to oneself) _____

8. (at) _____

9. (in the middle of) _____

10. (out of sight) _____

11. (to be in) _____

12. (out of) _____

13. (instead of) _____

14. (by) _____

15. (down-and-out) _____

Commonly Used Prepositions

aboard	concerning	opposite
about	considering	out
above	despite	out of
according to	down	outside
across	during	over
after	except	past
against	excluding	per
ahead of	following	regarding
along	for	round
amid	from	since
among	in	than
apart from	in back of	through
around	in front of	till
as	in reference to	to
at	in regard to	toward(s)
because of	in spite of	under
before	inside	underneath
behind	instead of	until
below	into	up
beneath	like	up to
beside	near	upon
between	of	with
beyond	off	with respect to
by	on	within
by means of	on account of	without
by way of	onto	

Answer Key

Part I Pronouns
Unit 1 Pronouns as the Subject of a Sentence

1-1
1. **She** has to go home at five o'clock.
2. When do **you** leave on your trip?
3. **They** were frightened during the storm.
4. **I** am planning on early retirement.
5. Why are **you** crying?
6. **Who** wants to arrange a surprise party for her?
7. **He** was sound asleep.
8. **What** needs to be repaired right away?
9. Where does **she** go every afternoon?
10. **They** earn a very good salary.

1-2
1. **She** is such a sweet child.
2. **They** just can't seem to get along.
3. Where did **they** find a place to rest?
4. **We** spent a week camping in the mountains.
5. **It** burned down last night.
6. Where is **he** from?
7. **They** roared overhead.
8. Why is **she** laughing?
9. Does **it** still hurt?
10. **We** can help you today.

1-3
1. Yes, I do. No, I don't.
2. Yes, she is. No, she isn't.
3. Yes, they have. No, they haven't.
4. Yes, he was. No, he wasn't.
5. Yes, you are. No, you aren't.
6. Yes, we are. No, we aren't.
7. Yes, she should. No, she shouldn't.
8. Yes, I can. No, I can't.
9. Yes, he should. No, he shouldn't.
10. Yes, they will. No, they won't.

Unit 2 Pronouns as Direct Objects

2-1
1. Why would the police want to arrest **us**?
2. My uncle visited **me** in Chicago.
3. Did the doctor ask **you** about the accident?
4. John caught **him** stealing a bicycle.
5. Can you join **us** for dinner?
6. I just can't believe **it**!
7. How can I reach **you** after you move?
8. The boys watched **her** all afternoon.

9. You can help **us** clean up the kitchen.
10. **Whom** should I call about a leaky faucet?

2-2

1. My sister liked **him** a lot.
2. Can you understand **it**?
3. I bought **them** at the mall.
4. When did you first meet **us**?
5. I spent **it**.
6. We used to visit **them** regularly.
7. I'd like to introduce **her**.

Unit 3 Pronouns as Indirect Objects

3-1

1. He won't sell **him** the car.
2. Did you bring **her** a gift?
3. I loaned **them** a hundred dollars.
4. Please give **her** a copy of the will.
5. I'm going to buy **them** some new pajamas.
6. James sent **her** a bouquet of roses.
7. She wrote **him** several letters.

3-2

1. I wanted to give **you** something nice.
2. Please send **her** a telegram with the news.
3. They brought **us** breakfast in bed.
4. Can you lend **me** a few dollars until tomorrow?
5. You ought to write **him** a letter every week.
6. She'll buy **you** new socks and underwear.
7. Mr. Brown gave **us** a lecture on politics again.
8. I'm sending **them** the directions to our new house.
9. Tell **me** a story.
10. Who bought **us** these tools?

Unit 4 Pronouns in a Prepositional Phrase

4-1

1. They were asking questions about **you**.
2. I received several letters from **her**.
3. From **whom** did you borrow the money?
4. **What** were they all laughing about?
5. Someone threw a rock at **me**.
6. This problem has nothing to do with **you**.
7. That shirt really looks good on **him**.
8. A crow was flying directly over **them**.
9. An old woman came up to **us**.
10. Those stories were written by **us**.

4-2

1. Three of the girls wanted to dance **with** me.
2. The artist painted a wonderful portrait **of** her.
3. **To** whom did you send the manuscript?
4. A little bird was sitting **on** it. (**near** it, **by** it, **with** it)
5. What did you put it **in**? (**near, on**)
6. I entered the building right **after** him.
7. There's a new bank **near** it. (**by** it)
8. The frightened dog came slowly up **to** us.

Unit 5 Direct and Indirect Object Pronouns in the Same Sentence

5-1

1. The magician showed **it to us**.
2. Don't give **them to the children**.
3. I can't lend **it to you**.
4. Who sent **it to your cousin**?
5. Tom is going to buy **it for them**.
6. The lawyer did **it for him**.
7. The lonely soldier wrote **them to his girlfriend**.
8. She gave **it to me**.
9. Uncle Robert bought **it for us**.
10. Do you send **it to them** every week?

5-2

1. The judge sent **them to them**.
2. Why did you show **it to her**?
3. I can't lend **it to him**.
4. Dr. Brown gave **them to her** (**him**).
5. Show **it to her** (**him**).
6. They're going to buy **them for him**.
7. Will you save **it for her**?

5-3

1. **They** were standing on the corner and laughing.
2. Someone threw **it** through that window!
3. Bill wants to buy **it** for her.
4. You shouldn't speak about **him** in that terrible way.
5. Where did you buy **it**?
6. Ms. Smith has moved out of **it**.
7. Do you know **them**?
8. **We** were on our way to the party when it happened.
9. I bought **them** for you.
10. Do you want to go there with **us**?
11. **She** has been elected chairperson of the committee.
12. He hates **them**.
13. Put **them** in the attic, please.
14. Is **he** the new boss?
15. We love **it**.

5-4

Sample Answers:
1. They met **me** in Chicago. Someone gave **me** ten dollars. Maria danced with **me**.
2. Do you know **her**? I sent **her** some flowers. I was thinking of **her**.
3. Mother introduced **us** to them. Jim bought **us** a hot dog. They got a letter from **us**.
4. The girl kissed **them**. Tom sent **them** a telegram. Did you speak with **them**?
5. **Whom** would you elect mayor? To **whom** did you give permission? From **whom** did they get these gifts?

Unit 6 Possessive Pronouns

6-1

1. **Her** brother goes to college.
2. Do you know **his** niece?
3. **Its** hole was behind a large rock.
4. **Their** chirping woke me up early.
5. She loved **her** solo.
6. I had to hold **her** purse.
7. **Her** piglets slept in a cool pile of mud.
8. Did you borrow **her** skis?
9. **Their** demands were too much for the company.
10. Where is **their** bed going to be?

6-2

1. I wanted to dance with **her** older sister.
2. Will you help me carry **my** books up to the second floor?
3. They said **your** father had been a colonel in the army.
4. **Our** tent was put up near a bend in the river.
5. Michael wanted to spend time at **our** campsite.
6. I still haven't met **their** parents.
7. **Whose** sailboat is that out on the lake?
8. I just can't get interested in **his** novels.
9. **Its** roof has been replaced with cedar shingles.
10. Ms. Garcia wanted to borrow **our** garden hose.

Unit 7 Demonstrative, Indefinite, and Interrogative Pronouns

7-1

1. I found **this** puppy behind a bush.
2. She thought **these** magazines were interesting.
3. **That** tall building is the city hall.
4. Would you like some of **these** nuts?
5. **Those** dark clouds mean a storm is coming.
6. **That** town is about two hundred miles from here.
7. Why do **those** people make so much noise?
8. I bought **this** necklace on sale.
9. **That** swing set is just for children.
10. **Those** boys played soccer all afternoon.

7-2

1. He has three brothers. **Each** served in the navy for three years.
2. I bought seven tickets. **All** were purchased at a discount.
3. The children didn't like her, and **none** would play with her.
4. **Nobody** put in enough time on the project.
5. **Everything** he said turned out to be a lie.
6. Many of them enjoyed the concert. **Others** went home early.
7. They invited a hundred guests. **Several** are already in the reception hall.
8. The two girls took part in the competition, but **neither** had a chance of winning.
9. **Anyone** found without proper identification will be arrested.
10. **Much** has been said about the problem, but nothing has been done.

7-3

1. **Who** would like to order some dinner?
2. **What** did she find in the drawer?
3. **Whose** is the fastest horse in the race?
4. **What** were they discussing?
5. **What** were several women talking about?
6. **Whom** did we meet while traveling in Mexico?
7. **Who** spent a lot of time in the mountains?
8. **What** do they prefer?
9. **What** slithered across the road?
10. From **whom** did they receive several letters?

Unit 8 Numbers as Pronouns

8-1

1. **Five** were playing in the mud.
2. I have **eleven** in that drawer.
3. **Two** are friends of mine.
4. **One** came from Ms. Garcia.
5. There were **five** on the table a moment ago.
6. The new sales clerk sold her **eight**.
7. **Three** applied for the same job.
8. There were at least **fifty** scattered about the floor.

Unit 9 The Pronoun *One*

1. **You** must have strength to carry on.
2. Should **you** always be on time for **your** lessons?
3. If **you lose your** wallet, **you** should report that to the police.
4. **You** ought to try to stay in shape.
5. When **you drink** too much, **you get** drunk
6. **You** have little choice when it comes to love.
7. **You** should always behave **yourself**.
8. How can **you** be so mean to her?
9. If **you have** too much time on **your** hands, **you need** to find a job.
10. When **you have** humility, **you** also **have** respect.

9-2

1. **One** might **get** into a lot of trouble. **You** might **get** into a lot of trouble.
2. If **one speaks** slowly, **one is** better understood. If **you speak** slowly, **you are** better understood.
3. **One ought** to consider taking the train there. **You ought** to consider taking the train there.
4. Should **one** criticize **one's** own mistakes? Should **you** criticize **your** own mistakes?
5. **One learns** slowly when **one is** very young. **You learn** slowly when **you are** very young.
6. In time, **one accepts one's** limitations. In time, **you accept your** limitations.
7. If **one carries on** like a fool, **one** will be considered a fool. If **you carry on** like a fool, **you** will be considered a fool.
8. When **one gets** a little too heavy, **one** should begin to exercise. When **you get** a little too heavy, **you** should begin to exercise.

Unit 10 Relative Pronouns

10-1

1. He found a puppy **that** needed a home.
2. Where did you put the groceries **that** I bought at the supermarket?
3. That's my car **that** has the convertible top.
4. There's the scientist **that** I told you about.
5. Do you know the woman **whose** son is serving in the army?
6. They hired the lawyer **that** they got the best deal from.
7. I need the map **that** has Cook County on it.
8. I was introduced to the girl **that** John was dancing with.
9. Don't spend the money **that** I put on the dresser.
10. Do you know the song **that** I'm playing on the piano?

1. I lost the book I got from Maria last week.
2. We like the dress, which was probably designed in Paris. (no change)
3. He read a sentence he can't understand at all.
4. I have all the documents I was speaking of.
5. Will you give me some money I can use to buy new underwear?
6. The champion, who is a native of Mexico, is touring the United States. (no change)
7. He bought a used car that had been in an accident. (no change)
8. Maria wants to use the umbrella Mom bought last week.
9. Do you understand the words I wrote on this sheet of paper?
10. I like Uncle Henry, from whom I received a beautiful gift. (no change)

10-3

Sample Answers:
1. Please show me the books **that you have for sale**.
2. I met the actor **who studied in Berlin**.
3. He bought a watch that **keeps perfect time**.
4. The boss, who **graduated from Harvard**, is rather nice.
5. Where are the gifts **that you received from Martha**?
6. This car, which **was recently repainted**, is from Germany.
7. I have the DVD **that came out just last month**.

Unit 11 Reflexive Pronouns

11-1
1. She sometimes writes stories about **herself**.
2. We really enjoyed **ourselves** very much.
3. My uncle cut **himself** with a sharp knife.
4. The ugly dragon hid **itself** behind a pile of stones.
5. I described **myself** honestly.
6. Would you recommend **yourself** for the job?
7. The girls saw **themselves** in the still water of the pond.
8. He didn't recognize **himself** in his new suit of clothes.
9. A young woman was admiring **herself** in the store window.
10. Maria and Juan! You've hurt **yourselves** again! Shame on you!

11-2
1. John believes himself to be innocent.
a. We believe ourselves to be innocent.
b. I believe myself to be innocent.
c. She believes herself to be innocent.
d. You believe yourselves to be innocent.
2. She considers herself lucky.
a. They consider themselves lucky.
b. I consider myself lucky.
c. You consider yourself lucky.
d. He considers himself lucky.

Unit 12 Reciprocal Pronouns

12-1
1. My father and mother sit next to one another.
2. The soprano and the tenor harmonize with one another.
3. The boys and the girls danced with each other.
4. My boss and the manager spoke about each other.
5. St. Paul and Minneapolis are located near one another.
6. Barbara and Juan kissed one another.
7. The lioness and the three cubs slept near one another.
8. You and I respect each other.
9. James and Maria sang for each other.
10. They like one another's voices.

12-2
Sample Answers:
1. (one another)
a. They love one another.
b. The boys and girls wouldn't play with one another.
c. Bob and Jim fought one another after school.
2. (each other)
a. We stared at each other.
b. Tom and I often helped each other.
c. They cared for each other's dogs.

Part II Prepositions
Unit 13 Prepositions That Indicate Location

13-1
1. A tiny rabbit was hiding **under** a bush.
2. Please don't sit **next to** me.
3. We saw several baby birds **in** a nest in that tree.
4. There was nothing **below** the plane but empty space.
5. Father stays **at** the factory until 5:00 P.M.

6. An angry man stood directly **in the middle of** us.
7. John stayed **beside** me the entire time.
8. I saw Maria **among** the many people at the party.
9. There was a huge bug sitting **on** my bed!
10. I saw a stranger crouching **between** my car and the truck.

13-2

Sample Answers:
1. I saw a jet flying above **the Rocky Mountains.**
2. Someone was hiding under **a large bush.**
3. Are you familiar with **the new family down the block**?
4. My sisters both work at **the new mall.**
5. The frightened kitten hid in **an old shoe box.**
6. Someone stood behind **the door and listened.**
7. Who was sitting among **the honored guests at the conference**?
8. There's nothing in front of **the broken-down SUV.**
9. Gray clouds hovered over **the dark forest.**
10. Have a seat next to **my mother-in-law.**
11. He found his keys on **the backseat of the car.**
12. I found a couple seats beside **the manager of the team.**
13. Let's set up our camp near **the bank of the river.**
14. We used to live between **the Miller family and old Mrs. Jones.**
15. A puppy sat lazily in the middle of **the freshly painted floor.**

13-3

Sample Answers:
1. We were on the train for over five hours.
2. I spend much too much time at work.
3. There was a mouse hiding behind the dresser.
4. Please take a seat next to her.
5. The elderly man is in the hospital again.
6. I like dancing with Maria.
7. I stood between them and stopped the fight.
8. An eagle was gliding over the mountains.
9. An angry bear stood up in front of us.
10. Grandfather slept under a palm tree.

Unit 14 Prepositions That Indicate Movement or Direction

14-1

1. The children ran **toward** the gate.
2. The young couple strolled **along** the beach.
3. The ball rolled **off** the table.
4. Is Thomas already **at** work?
5. I was hurrying **to** my desk.
6. Someone came running **into** the room.
7. We slowly drove **by** their house.
8. Ms. Brown came **from** England last year.
9. The poor girl fell **out of** bed.
10. I dropped the tools **into** the box.

14-2

Sample Answers:
1. The cattle were heading toward **a distant watering hole.**
2. Someone came out of **a dark corner of the room.**
3. Why were you going into **my private office**?
4. My family frequently travels to **the countryside of Mexico.**
5. Do you come from **Canada or the United States**?
6. The carpenter fell off **the steep roof.**
7. The burglar quietly climbed onto **the porch and reached for the window.**

8. Maria wants to come into **the dining room for a moment.**
9. The men were walking along **one of the beams of the building.**
10. He came at **his frightened victim** with a knife.
11. She drove by **our house** without stopping.
12. What time did you come home from **the rock concert?**
13. We're planning on traveling to **South America next year.**
14. The cat jumped into **my sister's lap.**
15. The woman moved cautiously toward **the open door.**

14-3

Sample Answers:
1. A little boy wandered along the shore.
2. The retired teacher drove by the school again.
3. She ran from the yard shouting.
4. Michael bolted into the living room and fell on the floor.
5. I threw a magazine onto the shelf.
6. The puppy fell off the bed.
7. The young driver slowly pulled out of the garage.
8. We've never traveled to the mountains.
9. The rabbit hopped toward the wall.
10. She was afraid of going into a darkened room.

Unit 15 Prepositions That Indicate Time

15-1

Sample Answers:
1. They left the theater **before** the end of the film.
2. I should be home **by** ten o'clock.
3. She only works **from** nine to three.
4. We always have a picnic **on** the Fourth of July.
5. Do you always eat lunch **at** noon?
6. Bill has been sad **since** his fortieth birthday.
7. Aunt Jane came to town **for** Carmen's big party.
8. We do a lot of shopping **during** the holiday season.
9. It's coldest here from December **to** February.
10. I'm afraid that we'll have to wait **until** tomorrow.

15-2

Sample Answers:
1. The children were very noisy during **the long meeting.**
2. We can expect Jim here for **your birthday party.**
3. It's very rainy from May to **August.**
4. I haven't seen you since **you were a little girl.**
5. Can you stay with me until **I finish this report?**
6. Tom works hard **from** morning to night.
7. They wanted to leave work before **their shift ended.**
8. The doctor gave him a checkup after **a long illness.**
9. Try to get here by **dusk.**
10. His family usually stays at the lake in **the summer months.**
11. The twins were born on **September fifth.**
12. Dark shadows covered the ground at **daybreak.**
13. They were living in Europe during **their youth.**
14. He's had a job in the city since **he came back from Mexico.**
15. They want to start the marathon by **twelve thirty.**

Sample Answers:

1. Her shift is from noon until midnight.
2. I hope to graduate by June.
3. We've been planting shrubs since the end of winter.
4. Tom returns home in spring.
5. The parade was on May tenth.
6. Quiet hours begin after 11:00 P.M.
7. I hope to finish the course before next year.
8. He's had many different jobs during his lifetime.
9. Uncle James got home after dark.
10. We usually sit on the porch at sunset.

Unit 16 Compound Prepositions

1. Some men stood **in front of** the store.
2. **According to** the forecast, it's going to rain today.
3. **In reference to** his remark, I just said, "Shame."
4. We stayed home **because of** the power outage.
5. Do you still live **in back of** the shop?
6. There **ahead of** us stood a large bison.
7. He quickly drove **out of** the driveway.
8. I was too nervous to walk **up to** the president.
9. It happened **on account of** your carelessness!
10. She can't comment **in regard to** that matter.

Sample Answers:

1. Please write a report in reference to **the latest sales figures**.
2. In spite of **his odd behavior**, she continued to love him.
3. In regard to **recent events**, I have a statement to make.
4. I bought a compact car instead of **a large SUV**.
5. Who's waiting in front of **that newsstand**?
6. The man was arrested on account of **several unpaid tickets**.
7. There were several tables and chairs in back of **the conference room**.
8. A strange smell came out of **the trash barrel**.
9. I sent her some flowers by way of **thanks for a great evening**.
10. A baby rabbit hopped up to **my foot and sniffed**.
11. You can get to the top of the mountain by means of **the aerial tramway**.
12. With respect to **our company's low morale**, some changes have to be made.
13. Apart from **two senior managers**, everyone else will be fired.
14. According to **the latest weather report**, we're in a heat wave.
15. I could see a winding road ahead of **us in the hills**.

Sample Answers:

1. Fortunately the bus arrived ahead of time.
2. She cancelled the trip because of an illness.
3. The strikers marched in front of the factory.
4. I have some comments in reference to your last report.
5. I paid with cash instead of a check.
6. A small plane flew out of the clouds.
7. With respect to his last wishes, a memorial service will be held tomorrow.
8. There will be a drought according to the almanac.
9. Apart from a few friends in Chicago, he knows no one in Illinois.
10. Travel is easiest by means of the subway.
11. You'll find a wheelbarrow in back of the garage.
12. In spite of the darkness, the carpenter continued his work.
13. He was only respected on account of his riches.
14. The hikers came up to the river.
15. I have something to say in regard to these lies.

Unit 17 Prepositions That Combine with Other Words

17-1

1. The strange woman was an **undercover** agent.
2. The newly elected governor is an **upstanding** person.
3. She **intoned** her voice with the anger she felt.
4. They decided to go **uptown** for dinner.
5. Did you follow our club's **bylaws**?
6. Her views just aren't **up-to-date**.
7. The hikers followed the creek **up-country**.
8. The old man didn't want to **outlive** his wife.
9. My aunt **underwent** a serious operation last year.
10. His look was **downcast** and his face quite sad.

17-2

Sample Answers:
1. The new members refused to follow the bylaws **of our organization**.
2. Out in the street there was an uproar over **a minor traffic accident**.
3. While swimming underwater, he saw **the outline of a boat**.
4. They were flying coach class but wanted to upgrade **to business class**.
5. An underage girl came into **the little tavern**.
6. The brothers were always trying to outdo **one another**.
7. The road uphill was **too steep for our little car**.
8. There was a sudden outbreak of **measles in our area**.
9. You need a technician to install **such complicated equipment**.
10. The downhearted young man began to **regret his decision to live alone**.
11. The couple lives downstairs from **a retired opera singer**.
12. The underclassmen in **our high school** behaved badly.
13. I didn't mean to upset **her relatives**.
14. The undercover agent hid **a package in a hollow tree trunk**.
15. Within hours there was a total downfall of **morale among the workers**.

17-3

Sample Answers:
1. The kids like playing outdoors.
2. This road leads to a bypass.
3. Dad intoned his words like a religious chant.
4. That ingrown toenail looks infected.
5. By and large, she's quite a nice person.
6. I have some further insight into the affair.
7. His underarms were wet with perspiration.
8. I bought some new underwear.
9. He drew up an outline for the manuscript.
10. The police are there to uphold the law.
11. There are several villages farther inland.
12. You have to go uptown to find a large bank.
13. The government fell because of an upheaval of the population.
14. I can't undergo another operation.
15. She's the most upstanding person in the legislature.

Unit 18 Participial Prepositions

18-1

1. We'll need to put in a lot of time **considering** this problem.
2. I had a lot to tell **concerning** the crimes he had committed.
3. I wanted to speak to her **regarding** our future together.
4. Maria passed every test **excluding** the one in math.
5. The picnic will go on as planned **following** the rainstorm.

18-2

Sample Answers:
1. I had the reports that were concerning your work here. He spoke for several minutes concerning the company's future.
2. I've been considering all your suggestions. He did a good job considering his lack of skill.
3. This club has been excluding women for years. He visited all the dealerships excluding the ones that sell foreign cars.
4. Someone is following us! He took a long shower following the two-hour workout.

Unit 19 Postpositive Prepositions

19-1

Sample Answers:
1. The pup fell over backward. He walked backward toward the door.
2. When I looked downward, I saw the footprints. The eagle swooped downward and targeted a rabbit.
3. Tomorrow we're homeward bound. The tourists eagerly headed homeward.
4. She looked inward for a reason for her behavior. Inwardly, he knew he couldn't believe the boy.
5. With a glance upward, he saw the missing package on a shelf. With an upward thrust, he knocked the man off his feet.
6. The lions moved windward so as not to leave a scent. Sailing vessels have difficulty sailing windward.
7. The refugees hiked eastward. An eastward wind meant that a storm was coming.

Unit 20 Words That Require a Specific Preposition

20-1

1. I began to beg my father **for** more money.
2. She was being followed **by** a strange man.
3. Juanita also **belongs** to our club now.
4. Don't you want to **ask** for a little help?
5. I never stop worrying **about** my daughter.
6. I really care **for** her. I'm in love.
7. Tom has absolutely no interest **in** jazz.
8. It's difficult for them to forget **about** the war.
9. I know I can **rely** on your honesty.
10. I **long** for a good night's sleep.
11. She was deeply hurt **by** his insults.
12. The child is hardly capable **of** hurting anyone.
13. I'll **wait** for you in front of the theater.
14. You shouldn't be so generous **with** us.
15. Are you looking forward **to** the party?

20-2

Sample Answers:
1. He became alarmed by **the patient's condition**.
2. You shouldn't worry about **unimportant things**.
3. These women are very interested in **computer science**.
4. I'm going to wish for **a brand new car**.
5. Are you absolutely sure of **the doctor's diagnosis**?
6. The immigration officer walked up to **the last applicant in line**.
7. Does this jacket belong to **anyone here**?
8. You're always thinking about **other people**.
9. How can I depend on **a man like Jim**?
10. The wounded soldier was pleading for **release from his pain**.
11. Never forget about **what happened to me**.
12. The barn was blown down by **a sudden northern gale**.
13. We need a guard to watch over **the shipment that just came in**.
14. You should listen to **your elders**.
15. A large animal was looking at **me from out of the brush**.

20-3

1. The young man **came up to** me with a gift in his hand.
2. The orator **spoke about** the importance of saving money.
3. I think this umbrella **belonged** to Aunt Norma.
4. I **forgot about** the exam! I'm going to fail for sure!
5. If you needed anything, you always **depended (relied) on** me.
6. A police officer **cared for** the injured pedestrian.
7. Where were you? I **waited for** you for two hours!
8. Dad **worried about** me, but I knew how to take care of myself.
9. The boys **looked for** the missing child for several hours.
10. Jim **begged (pleaded) for** an extra ten dollars but got nothing.

20-4

Sample Answers:
1. You're capable of better work than this.
2. She was looking for her keys.
3. The tree was struck by lightning.
4. I have no interest in that man.
5. It's silly to wish for things.
6. The mother made a plea for her son's life.
7. I'm sure of what I saw.
8. You know you can rely upon my word.
9. The pup sat up and begged for the bone.
10. Anita is looking forward to her date with Jim.
11. I don't care about ancient history.
12. Barbara hoped for a chance to be on the team.
13. The flight attendant looked after the passengers' needs.
14. I dream of becoming a jet pilot.
15. They were motivated by their greed.

Unit 21 Prepositions and Phrasal Verbs

21-1

1. It's cold. The heat **is** probably off.
2. If you ask **around**, you'll get his address.
3. The old woman was **up to** something again.
4. She was too timid to **ask** Juan out.
5. The scientist knew she was **onto** something.
6. My lawyer won't be **in** until noon.
7. Your parents are so up-to-date and **with it**.
8. Why was the TV **on** all night?
9. The detective believed she was up **to no good**.
10. He wants to take a shower but the water is **off** again.

21-2

1. I wanted to know who he was and **asked around** about him.
2. The jumbo jet was quickly **out of sight**.
3. The burglar was obviously **up to** no good.
4. What time will Professor Gomez **be** in?
5. Did your nephew **ask** my niece out?
6. Having found a clue, they knew they were **onto something**.
7. If the fan **is on**, why is it so hot in here?
8. When he turned to look, her train was already out **of sight**.
9. Use makeup! Color your hair! Try to be **with it**!
10. The dentist is **out (in)** for the day.

21-3

1. Jim came through **for** me again.
2. Let's get on **with** the meeting.
3. The drowsy woman came **to** very slowly.
4. The children came **upon** a little cottage in the woods.
5. I work all afternoon. I get **off** at 5:00 P.M.
6. Ms. Brown **came up** with a wonderful slogan.
7. Hurry! You're **getting** behind in your work.
8. How can I get **in on** this deal?
9. The two boys got **into it** after school.
10. She got **back at** us for gossiping.

21-4

1. Start the music. Let's get **on with** the show.
2. I don't want to stay in jail! Please **get** me off!
3. Mr. Brown finally **came up** with our loan.
4. They were arguing over the accident and soon **got into** it.
5. Maybe she'll come **to** if you give her some water.
6. Jim **came upon** an old magazine in the attic.
7. Did Maria get **in on** the stock purchase?
8. We all **got behind** Ms. Brown, and she won the election.
9. The car dealer eventually came through **for** us.
10. I **get off** at six. You can pick me up then.

21-5

1. You run too fast. I can't keep **up with** you.
2. With one blow, he knocked the man **out**.
3. We have to **keep on** working until we're done.
4. The landlord kicked us **out of** our apartment.
5. Knock **it** off. You're bothering me.
6. The carpenters **knocked down** the wall in just a few minutes.
7. They kicked **off** the parade with a patriotic march.
8. He was shot in the morning. He kicked **off** in the afternoon.
9. What time do you knock **off** work?
10. She's so lonely, yet she still keeps **to herself**.

21-6

1. The coach wanted them to **keep on** practicing.
2. Careful or you'll knock **out** the window!
3. How can we keep those kids **out of** our yard?
4. You had better knock **it off** before I get really angry.
5. If you keep **to** this road, you'll get there in an hour.
6. They had an argument, and she **kicked** him out.
7. The champ knocked his opponent **down**, but he got up immediately.
8. If you pedal faster, you'll **keep up** with the other cyclists.
9. We'll **kick** off the party with a few drinks.
10. What time do you **knock off** of work?

21-7

1. Put me **down** for the refreshments committee.
2. The baby is feverish and won't **quiet** down.
3. I need to rest up **from** all this exercise.
4. Carmen **put up with** his lies for many years.
5. You're so hospitable, but don't **put yourself** out.
6. He's so excited, but he needs to quiet **down**.
7. I **rested up** all morning and went to work at noon.
8. She's not sick! She's just putting **on**!
9. It can't be true! Are you **putting** me on?
10. The janitor was **put out by** all the garbage in the hallway.

21-8

1. Why don't you **rest up**? You've had a long day.
2. You're never satisfied with my work. You always **put** me down.
3. Spend the night here. We can put you **up**.
4. When the class **quiets** down, I'll pass out the new material.
5. I love soccer. Put me **down for** that team.
6. Tom **put on** a dress and a wig for the Halloween party.
7. Anita can't put **up with** his deceit any longer.
8. I think you should rest **up from** that long trip.
9. He wished he could put his roommate **out of** his house.
10. You can put the groceries **down on** that table.

21-9

1. Ms. Brown will take over **from** Mr. Jones.
2. Let's sit down and talk this problem **over**.
3. I took everything **back from** her apartment.
4. You shouldn't **talk back** to your mother!
5. You're not going to talk me **into** that again.
6. I'll take **down** the curtains and wash them.
7. The shelter **takes in** homeless people.
8. Take **off** your coat and relax.
9. That skirt is long. Let's take it **up**.
10. My brother **took up** with my ex-girlfriend.

21-10

1. A new company took **over** the factory.
2. His store is **taking on** several new employees.
3. **Talking** back to a teacher is terrible behavior.
4. In the summer the students took off **for** California
5. Your waist is smaller. You should take **in** your pants.
6. I'd like to take you **up on** your offer.
7. Anita **talked** me into going to the dance with her.
8. The reporter took **down** every word I said.
9. You ought to **take back** what you said to her.
10. No one talked it **over** with me.

21-11

1. Grandmother put on **an apron**.
2. We need to talk **it** over.
3. I can't put up with **your insults**.
4. They'll kick off **the celebration** at ten o'clock.
5. We're going to take in **some boarders**.
6. The drug knocked **her** out.
7. Mr. Johnson took over **our business**.
8. Put **the gun** down and turn around.
9. I'll measure the skirt and you take **it** in.
10. We need to quiet **your mother** down.

21-12

Sample Answers:
1. She knocked the thief down. She knocked down the thief. She knocked him down.
2. Help put the tents up. Help put up the tents. Help put them up.
3. Norma took the company over. Norma took over the company. Norma took it over.
4. The fireman kicked the window out. The fireman kicked out the window. The fireman kicked it out.
5. She puts the baby down for a nap. She puts down the baby for a nap. She puts her down for a nap.
6. Let's take the old carpet up. Let's take up the old carpet. Let's take it up.
7. Can you quiet the kids down? Can you quiet down the kids? Can you quiet them down?
8. Don't knock the vase off. Don't knock off the vase. Don't knock it off.

Unit 22 A Variety of Prepositional Uses

22-1
1. We've been living in this house **since** last March.
2. Coach is filled, but I can **upgrade** you to first class.
3. The security guard **watched over** the new shipment of computers.
4. The electricity **has been off** for two days.
5. I often dream **about** my home in Ireland.
6. The frightened dog had been bitten **by** a snake.
7. The Constitution was finally ratified **on** this date.
8. I enjoy it here **in spite of** the bad weather.
9. There's a newspaper boy **at** the front door.
10. We really look **forward to** your next visit.

22-2
Sample Answers:
1. Why do you spend so much time with **such rude people**?
2. Several fans came rushing up to **the rock star**.
3. Who asked for **a Coke and a hamburger**?
4. I usually get off **at half past eight**.
5. I learned not to depend upon **anyone but myself**.
6. They should be in Detroit on **New Year's Day**.
7. The ship docked at **5:00 P.M.**
8. Maria can't seem to forget about **her ex-boyfriend**.
9. The sleek sailboat headed seaward and **then set a course for Bermuda**.
10. The new golf clubs belong to **the boss's wife**.
11. My relatives will return to New York in **two weeks**.
12. I haven't been in Europe since **the fall of 2002**.
13. Did you remain in the United States during **the gas crisis**?
14. According to **the local newspaper**, there's going to be a storm today.
15. Somehow the new employee came up with **a very clever idea**.
16. The embarrassed girl decided to get back at **the boy who played a trick on her**.
17. Our flight arrived ahead of **schedule**.
18. I don't like waiting for **food deliveries**.
19. **The dog's snarling** upset the poor woman.
20. **Lazy cattle were grazing** in the pasture.
21. **The giant dirigible** was soon out of sight.
22. **The captain of the soccer team** wanted to belong to our fraternity.
23. **A disruptive visitor was shown** out of the conference hall.
24. Apart from my own parents, **no one came to see me in the play**.
25. **The horse and carriage clattered** toward the covered bridge.

22-3
Sample Answers:
1. Throw a log onto the fire.
2. We crashed into a tree because of a deer.
3. I don't know what I want to do after college.
4. We were heading homeward when we decided to go to Las Vegas instead.
5. He was making some notes concerning the debate about pollution.
6. Are you interested in botany?
7. Jim likes keeping to himself.
8. Someone was standing at the window and looking in.
9. Don't interrupt me when I'm in the middle of a sentence.
10. He went over the top of the hill and was out of sight.
11. Is my attorney in today?
12. She jumped out of the closet and startled him.
13. I'll have a cheeseburger instead of the pizza.
14. This portrait was painted by Rembrandt.
15. The poor man was down-and-out and had no place to go.